TIME
MANAGEMENT

TIME
MANAGEMENT

A Catholic Approach

By Marshall J. Cook

auline
BOOKS & MEDIA
Boston

Library of Congress Cataloging-in-Publication Data

Cook, Marshall, 1944-
  Time management : a Catholic approach / by Marshall J. Cook.
     p. cm.
  ISBN 0-8198-7429-9 (pbk.)
  1. Time management—Religious aspects—Catholic Church. I. Title.
  BV4598.5.C66 2009
  248.4—dc22
                              2009019032

Cover design by Rosana Usselmann

Cover photo: MBPHOTO / istockphoto.com

Published by Pauline Books & Media, 50 Saint Paul's Avenue, Boston, MA 02130-3491

Printed in the U.S.A.

www.pauline.org

Pauline Books & Media is the publishing house of the Daughters of St. Paul, an international congregation of women religious serving the Church with the communications media.

1 2 3 4 5 6 7 8 9   13 12 11 10 09

Contents

Part 1

CAN WE REALLY "MANAGE" TIME?

Part 2

HOW TO CONTROL CHRONOS TIME

Part 3

KEEPING THE SABBATH HOLY

.

Introduction

The Habit of Hurry

Jack LaLanne, pioneering fitness enthusiast, hosted a nationally syndicated television program from 1951 until 1985. He preached the virtues of exercise and good nutrition decades before Richard Simmons tried to get America "sweatin' to the oldies."

Each year on his birthday LaLanne would perform some incredible feat of strength and endurance to demonstrate how well his regimen worked. On his seventieth birthday, LaLanne held a towrope in his teeth and plunged into the late-summer waters of San Francisco Bay towing seventy rowboats carrying seventy people—and he was handcuffed and shackled when he did it!

Is that how an average day feels to you? You're towing too many rowboats full of too much dead weight; you're bound hand and foot; and if you relax for even a moment, you'll drown. You swim as hard as you can from the moment you wake up until you finally tumble into bed, exhausted but unable to sleep because you know that in a few short hours the alarm clock will set the agony into motion all over again.

You just might be trying to haul too many rowboats. To all the demands of job and family, you've added your obligations to church and community. All the things on your to-do list are fully worthy of your time and energy, but taken together, they leave you exhausted, frustrated, and consumed by a goading sense of failure.

Even when you are not pressed by an immediate deadline, the habit of hurry may keep you running from dawn to well past dusk.

If you see yourself in this description, applying principles of values-based time management can help you.

The Pocket God

If you think time flies now, be glad you weren't living in England in 1752 when the Gregorian calendar came into use. To make everything fit, eleven full days had to simply disappear. When folks went to bed, it was September 2, but when they woke up, it was September 14. (Had I been alive then, I would have had my birthday stolen from me, a fate well known to anyone born on February 29.)

But people didn't really "lose" those days, just as we don't really lose an hour when we "spring forward" each year to try to fool the sun into staying up later. Nothing really changes. We just reset the calibration on the instrument we use to keep track of the elusive abstraction we call time. It doesn't make any difference to the movement of the planets whether we're on daylight saving time or standard time or Howdy Doody Time. Hours by any other name would pass just as quickly, we'd never feel we had enough of them, and we'd still be driven to try to fill them beyond their capacity.

In Jonathan Swift's scathing political satire, *Gulliver's Travels*, the Lilliputians conclude that Gulliver's pocket watch must be his god, since he consults it before making any decision. Today an observer might conclude that our triune god is the PDA, the cell phone, and the holy laptop computer.

Instead of consulting these modern "gods" of technology for wisdom in planning how to spend our time, let's pause for a moment and look to the Master for guidance. As busy as we may be, can any of us claim to be busier than Jesus was during his brief time on earth? He had only three years to accomplish his mission, which was nothing less than the salvation of the human race. People made incessant demands on his time. As word of his miraculous healings spread, those seeking his teaching and his touch besieged him constantly.

For every person he healed—for every cripple who picked up his mat and walked, for every blind woman who opened her eyes and saw, for every possessed soul freed from its demons—there must have been hundreds more Jesus never got to. There was only one of him and so many of them, so much suffering, so much need. There just wasn't enough time to cure them all.

Yet Jesus never seemed to hurry. He never complained of being too busy. Instead, he always had time to explain things to the disciples, to share a meal, to feed the multitudes, to linger with people, like the woman at the well. He accepted "interruptions" as the Father's call to service. No matter the demands on his time, he always made time to be alone with the Father in prayer.

He was living on God's time, not man's.

> That evening, at sundown, they brought to him all who were sick or possessed with demons. And the whole city was gathered around the door. And he cured many who were sick with various diseases, and cast out many demons; and he would not permit the demons to speak, because they knew him.
>
> In the morning, while it was still very dark, he got up and went out to a deserted place, and there he prayed. And Simon and his companions hunted for him. (Mk 1:32–36)

When the end of his brief ministry on earth drew near, he didn't lament the lack of time or bemoan the work left undone. Instead, he expressed satisfaction with what he had accomplished. "I glorified you on earth by finishing the work that you gave me to do. So now, Father, glorify me in your own presence with the glory that I had in your presence before the world existed" (Jn 17:4).

Whose Time Is It?

Time, which is to say life, is a gift from God. Every day the loving Father gives us twenty-four hours, 1,440 minutes, to do with as we choose. We rush to consume those minutes, trying to fill them with as much activity as we possibly can.

In the creation narrative in Genesis, God made heaven and earth and put lights in the heavens to mark the days—all before he made us. Each day began with sunset, so Adam and Eve awoke to a day already in progress. God provided for a time for them to lie down and rest, and he set aside one day each week to devote fully to rest and regeneration. This was God's time and God's rhythm for creation.

The world didn't depend on Adam and Eve any more than it depends on us. Everything depends on God. We can claim no credit for our own existence. There are no "self-made" men or women. He gives us life, and we live for exactly as long as he wills it and not one second longer.

God gives each of us an equal allotment of time each day. We can't save it, kill it, waste it, or spend it. We can only *live* it, wisely or foolishly, for the greater glory of the God who made us or for some other, lesser reason. When we understand this, we also understand that this day, this moment, this eternal *now* is all we have—and all we'll ever need.

In this little book, we'll examine ways we can live in this miraculous *now* more fully alive to God's presence and his unending love for us. I'll encourage you to organize your activities and apply good principles of time management, but I'll also encourage you to slow down. If you do, you'll find you actually have more time and greater freedom in how you spend it.

First we'll examine our cultural concept of time and compare it with the sense of God's time we get from evaluating the Scriptures. We'll develop our awareness of *kairos* time, the right and proper time for every activity under God's heaven. We'll contrast the natural rhythms of creation with the speed sickness that grips our culture and puts us out of step with God and our own best selves. We'll look closely at God's advice to us in Scripture on how to manage our time and why we need to.

In the second section of the book, we'll get down to specifics—techniques for corralling *chronos* time: the minutes, hours, and days that comprise our lives. In Chapter 5, Moment Management, we'll learn how to make each decision only once, and we'll practice saying no to activities that distract us from our real goals. We'll explore ten tips for constructing our to-do lists—and learn why we also need to create *not*-to-do lists.

Subsequent chapters will offer suggestions for dealing with the demands technology places on our time and energy. We will develop strategies for processing and evaluating the flood of information that engulfs us, so we can keep from drowning in that flood. We'll glory in the power of the pause, turning an unwanted wait into a refreshing wait. We'll deal with time wasters, and pare unnecessary and unwanted activities from our lives. And we'll master the simple mathematics of time management, the fundamental substitution principle that allows us to take on new activities without trying to manufacture extra hours in the day.

In the third and final section of the book, we'll focus on the first day of the week, the Sabbath, and God's command to keep it holy. We'll review the scriptural basis for this commandment and Pope John Paul II's teaching on how we are to follow it, beginning with his definition of each Sunday as a "little Easter." We'll come to understand more fully the need for communal as well as private prayer.

We'll see how Jesus fulfilled rather than abolished the law of the Sabbath. We'll look at the obligatory nature of our attendance at weekly Mass and also seize on each "holy day of opportunity" to attend weekday Masses.

But if you decide to start attending weekday Mass, or to add any other activity to your schedule, doesn't that mean you must somehow try to squeeze still more into an already overstuffed schedule? It won't require squeezing, because you'll know how to make the time for Mass—or for any other activity you decide to take on as part of your God-centered time management. You'll be managing *chronos* time by living in *kairos* time, God's right time.

Part 1

Can We Really "Manage" Time?

Chapter 1

God's Time and Our Time

If he could "put time in a bottle," Jim Croce sang, he'd save every day so he could spend eternity with his ladylove. It's a lovely, romantic notion—but quite fanciful. We can't really "save" time.

But we sure talk as if we could.

We speak of saving time, wasting time, and spending time, some of it that elusive "quality time." We even equate time with money.

Our approach to time is probably a lot closer to poet Andrew Marvell's than to balladeer Croce's. Marvell, you may remember, attempted to seduce in his poem "To His Coy Mistress" with this line of reasoning:

> Had we but world enough, and time,
> This coyness, lady, would be no crime….

Ah, but we don't have "world enough and time," Marvell warns. Instead:

> But at my back I always hear
> Time's winged chariot hurrying near.

Another poet in a rush, Robert Herrick, apparently heard that chariot, too. In his poem "To the Virgins, to Make Much of Time," he advised all coy maidens to:

> Gather ye rosebuds while ye may,
> Old Time is still a-flying;

> And this same flower that smiles today
> Tomorrow will be dying.

Like the poets, we feel a crushing sense of urgency, tell one another we're too busy, and complain that there just aren't enough hours in a day. We dash off to the next appointment on the schedule, talking on the cell phone as we speed through a yellow light. We're trapped in the frenzy of the moment, trying to outrun the past and catch the future.

We've developed the habit of hurry, even though we really do have "world enough and time" in God, who was, is, and always will be. "[W]ith the Lord one day is like a thousand years, and a thousand years are like one day" (2 Pet 3:8).

Understanding God's Time

God chose to send his Son to live among us in a culture and an age that had no watches or modern-style clocks and lived by a vastly different perception of time from ours.

The original Hebrew and Greek texts of the Bible use many words to represent our single word "time." In Hebrew, time could be *ayt*, the moment in which something takes place; or *olam*, immeasurable time beyond all human comprehension; or *mo 'ed*, the fixed or appointed time designed for a specific event.

In Greek, we find *chronos*, chronological time, and *kairos*, God-given time, the proper time. *Kairos* is the acceptable time of which Saint Paul speaks, the time of opportunity, the fullness of time:

> As we work together with him, we urge you also not to accept the grace of God in vain.
>> For he says,
>> "At an acceptable time I have listened to you.
>> and on a day of salvation I have helped you."
>> See, now is the acceptable time; see, now is the day of salvation! (2 Cor 6:1–2)

Paul uses *kairos* some thirty times in his letters, and the word appears on at least fifty more occasions in the New Testament.

The most often cited formulation of this sense of "right time" comes from the Old Testament, at the beginning of the third chapter of Ecclesiastes:

> For everything there is a season, and a time for every matter under heaven:
>> a time to be born, and a time to die;
>> a time to plant, and a time to pluck up what is planted;
>> a time to kill, and a time to heal;
>> a time to break down, and a time to build up;
>> a time to weep, and a time to laugh;
>> a time to mourn, and a time to dance;
>> a time to throw away stones, and a time to gather stones together;
>> a time to embrace, and a time to refrain from embracing;
>> a time to seek, and a time to lose;
>> a time to keep, and a time to throw away;
>> a time to tear, and a time to sew;
>> a time to keep silence, and a time to speak;
>> a time to love, and a time to hate;
>> a time for war, and a time for peace. (Eccl 3:1–8)

In the New Testament, *kairos* can refer to the time of salvation and the time when darkness rules the earth. We must live through the dark *kairos* to reach the salvation *kairos*. The day of the Christ's return is near. "For salvation is nearer to us now than when we became believers; the night is far gone, the day is near" (Rom 13:11–12).

God has made his will known to us "according to his good pleasure that he set forth in Christ, as a plan for the fullness of time, to gather up all things in him, things in heaven and things on earth" (Eph 1:9–10).

Jesus had an acute sense of the right time, the ordained time. But his mother actually gave the signal when it was time for his public ministry to begin, at the wedding feast in Cana. When Mary told her son that the host had run out of wine, he replied: "Woman, what concern is that to you and to me? My hour has not yet come" (Jn 2:4). But she told the servants to do whatever Jesus told them, and moments later, he changed water into the finest wine.

"Jesus did this, the first of his signs, in Cana of Galilee, and revealed his glory; and his disciples believed in him" (Jn 2:11).

Jesus also indicated when the time was not yet right for him to reveal himself fully as the Messiah. When he healed the leper, the first of his ten early miracles chronicled in Matthew, he admonished the man, "See that you say nothing to anyone" (Mt 8:4). A little farther along his journey, he restored sight to two blind men, again warning, "See that no one knows of this" (Mt 9:30).

His friends urged him in John 7:2–10 to blow his cover at the time of the Sukkot, the Jewish festival of booths. "'Leave here and go to Judea so that your disciples also may see the works you are doing, for no one who wants to be widely known acts in secret. If you do these things, show yourself to the world.'"

But Jesus replied, "My time has not yet come."

In Matthew 4:17, as his ministry began, the time had not yet come for Jesus to reveal his nature, but by Matthew 16:21, it was time for Jesus to explain to his disciples what was going to happen to him. He announced the right time for the harvest in John 4: "Do you not say, 'Four months more, then comes the harvest'? But I tell you, look around you, and see how the fields are ripe for harvesting" (Jn 4:35).

His miracles soon became public, of course, most notably with the multiplication of the loaves and fishes. His most dramatic pronouncement of his messianic mission came after he proclaimed the words of the prophet Isaiah:

> "The Spirit of the Lord is upon me,
> because he has anointed me to bring good news to the
> 　　poor.
> He has sent me to proclaim release to the captives
> and recovery of sight to the blind, to let the oppressed
> 　　go free,
> to proclaim the year of the Lord's favor." (Lk 4:18–19)

> And he rolled up the scroll, gave it back to the attendant, and sat down. The eyes of all in the synagogue were fixed on him. Then he began to say to them, "Today this scripture has been fulfilled in your hearing." (Lk 4:21)

We are to be vigilant in watching for the proper time of salvation. "When you see a cloud rising in the west, you immediately say, 'It is going to rain'; and so it happens," Jesus tells the crowds in Luke 12:54. "You hypocrites! You know how to interpret the appearance of earth and sky, but why do you not know how to interpret the present time?" (Lk 12:56).

Although the New Testament narrative in general and Christ's parables in particular draw on the circular rhythms of the seasons, Biblical time is clearly linear, with key events occurring only once, at the appointed time, moving God's creation toward salvation. The birth, death, and resurrection of the Christ are the central events, of course, singular, memorialized in the Church calendar, and embodied in the Eucharist.

God gives us our allotted span of time and guides our destinies.

> You turn us back to dust, and say, "Turn back, you mortals."
> For a thousand years in your sight are like yesterday when it
> 　　is past,
> or like a watch in the night.
> You sweep them away; they are like a dream. . .

> The days of our lives are seventy years,
>   or perhaps eighty, if we are strong. (Ps 90:3–5, 10)

God is the author of time (see Gen 1:5), the ruler of history. Everything happens in God's appointed time.

"So teach us to count our days that we may gain a wise heart" (Ps 90:12).

Kairos (right time) is aligned with *kalos*, that which is inherently good and beautiful. In Luke 8:15, Jesus admonishes us that when we hear the word of God, we should "hold it fast in an honest and good [*kalos*] heart."

"[H]old fast," Paul tells us in 1 Thessalonians 5:21, "to what is good" (*kalos*).

Seeking a Values-Based Time Management

If Adam and Eve had watches and calendars, or even a concept of time beyond the cycle of sunrise and sunset and the changing of the seasons, the Bible doesn't mention it. They ate when they were hungry, slept when they were tired, and literally let nature take its course. It sounds great, doesn't it? It should. Before the Fall, Adam and Eve lived in paradise, after all, and they daily walked with God.

But in our fallen state, evil competes with good for our time and attention. We must love goodness and resist evil, choose life and not death. We must earn our keep by the sweat of our brows (although many of us now sweat at work only when nervous or when the air conditioning breaks down).

Along with and perhaps to help alleviate the pressures of work, we've developed myriad entertainments with which to divert ourselves. All this activity creates the "not enough hours in the day" syndrome. If we don't somehow manage all the conflicting demands on our time, others will manage them for us and will make our choices for us. We'll feel compelled by every seeming emergency and every sparkling desire our modern world can throw at us. Our lives will be up for grabs, with friend, neighbor, boss, enemy, huckster, politician, and reigning American idol all demanding our attention.

They call shrilly and incessantly. God calls in a still, small voice. How are we to hear, let alone heed him? What criteria do we use to allocate the precious 1,440 minutes he gives us each day?

Our decisions must begin by acknowledging that our lives belong to God. Prayer must guide them. And they must be rooted in an honest appraisal of our lives and a sincere desire to love and serve God. We must maintain a clear sense of our mission on earth: to love God and love our neighbor. Everything flows from this.

> He had told you, O mortal, what is good; and what does the LORD require of you / but to do justice, and to love kindness, and to walk humbly with your God?" (Mic 6:8)

God calls us to discern the *kalos* in our lives and live it in thought, word, and deed.

Separating the Important from the Merely Urgent

Stephen Covey stressed the importance of values-based time management in his book *First Things First*. In this book, he develops four categories we can use to classify all our activities on the basis of their importance and urgency. As the prophet Micah indicates, an important activity contributes to our mission to do justice, love kindness, and walk humbly with God. An urgent activity needs to be done quickly, if not immediately.

Covey challenges us to separate all our actions into one of four categories:

- ○ Important and urgent
- ○ Important but not urgent
- ○ Urgent but not important
- ○ Neither urgent nor important

When we look at our activities through this lens, we may discover that we spend too much time on the "urgent but not important" and not enough time on the "important but not urgent." An example of "urgent but not important" might be rushing to get to a meeting on time—only to wonder for the next two hours why you went at all. Into the "important but not urgent" area might fall most of the really good stuff, such as spending time with loved ones and nourishing friendships. It also includes the stuff we know we need to do but never seem to get around to, such as developing a regular exercise regimen or long-range financial planning.

In this list, I place possible activities into their proper categories. You could make your own list, to reflect your life.

IMPORTANT AND URGENT

- ○ Your child is sick or injured at school.
- ○ You have a big presentation and only two hours to prepare.
- ○ A car swerves in front of you on the highway.
- ○ Your water breaks!

IMPORTANT BUT NOT URGENT

- ○ Getting regular exercise.
- ○ Reading that great novel or inspirational book.
- ○ Spending time with family.
- ○ Praying.
- ○ Studying Scripture.

URGENT BUT (MOST LIKELY) NOT IMPORTANT

○ A colleague needs a "minute" to talk.

○ The department meeting started four minutes ago.

○ Your e-mail icon is blinking.

○ The phone is ringing—at dinnertime—again.

NEITHER URGENT NOR IMPORTANT

○ Working the daily crossword puzzle.

○ Catching up on office gossip.

○ Reading the baseball box scores (it hurt me to list this one).

○ Edging the lawn (I made up for that last one by including this one).

The "important and urgent" events require no decision-making, no time management. We don't schedule a convenient time to go pick up the child who's desperately sick at school. We drop everything and go.

The "not important/not urgent" stuff doesn't need a lot of thought, either, but that doesn't mean we should automatically cut it out of our lives. It's okay to do things just for the fun of it. Otherwise, as the character Murray Burns puts it so eloquently in the play *A Thousand Clowns*, life can become one long dental appointment. But when time gets scarce, these can be the first items you jettison from your overburdened life.

The remaining two categories are the ones that require work. We may need to take time from "urgent but not important" and give it to "important but not urgent." This is the essence of good time management.

Two important and urgent tasks may demand our attention at the same time, or we may simply run out of time to do both. The early disciples faced such a dilemma when they found themselves without sufficient time to preach the Gospel of the risen Christ and provide for the temporal needs of the community. They solved the problem by empowering more disciples to share the load (see Acts 6:1–7).

When we face such tough choices, we seek God's guidance, adhering always to the principle to "strive first for the kingdom of God and his righteousness" (Mt 6:33). We Catholics don't simply "manage" our time; we express our stewardship over the precious life the Father gives us. With this in mind, we'll reflect in the second section of this book on specific techniques for making good decisions regarding time. But first, let's spend a bit more time examining the obstacles we face, especially the social epidemic of "speed sickness," which fosters the habit of hurry and can create some truly awful symptoms.

CHAPTER 2

Recovering from Speed Sickness

"It was the best of times; it was the worst of times," Charles Dickens famously began his novel, *A Tale of Two Cities*. "Whether it's the best of times or the worst of times, it's the only time we've got," humorist Art Buchwald added decades later.

Most of us feel that we don't have enough time, good or bad, but lack of time may not always be the problem.

According to one estimate, the average American will spend fifty hours a week working, forty-five sleeping, and fifteen eating. Five hours a week go to shopping. We'll spend two hours for exercise and just one for religious and volunteer activities.

What about that extra fifty hours per week left unaccounted for? We're watching television. The same source estimates that, by age fifty, the average American will have spent eleven years (!) parked in front of the tube. That's close to five hours a day. I hope the estimate is high, but I'm not so sure.

You'd think we'd feel awfully relaxed with all that chilling out in front of the television. But we don't. We pressure ourselves constantly. We worship work and constant busyness. We display a compulsion to produce and perform. We strive for power, prestige, and possessions. These earthly desires "wage war against the soul," Peter warns us (1 Pet 2:11), even as they consume the hours of our days and the days of our lives. We can never get enough.

Even our play has become utilitarian. We "rest" so we can be more effective when we work, and our vacations become checklists of tasks to accomplish and places to go. The fear of wasting time invades every moment, dominating our lives and robbing us of the ability to enjoy God's creation.

In our frenzy to do things, we often lose track of why we're doing them. We're like the motorist who doesn't care what he's missing, as long as he's making good time. Like Mr. Toad in the *Wind in the Willows*, we're "merrily on our way to nowhere in particular."

We chase speed for speed's sake, and time management becomes a matter of trying to cram more activity into the same limited, nonelastic time through techniques like multitasking and learning how to brush off "time-wasting" people.

Why this obsession with perpetual motion? I'll offer five reasons. You can no doubt supply others.

Reason 1: *Greed*

We want money, power, praise, and prestige; when we get them, we want more. Of course, we're not talking about people who are forced to work two or even three jobs just to pay the rent and put food on the table.

Reason 2: *Vanity*

We're more concerned with pleasing people than God. Colleagues may ridicule the notion of spending time in worship and meditation; many see religion as a crutch or a drug for the weak. On the other hand, folks admire us for working long hours, proving our "dedication."

Reason 3: *Ego*

Our work is *so* important, and only *we* can do it right.

Reason 4: *Yes-itis*

As an outgrowth of ego and vanity, we never learn to say no. We want to please everyone, to be all things to all people.

Reason 5: *Fear*

We get hopelessly busy with certain tasks so we can avoid other, more important or more difficult ones. We embrace the familiar and shun the new. Consider the man who is master of all that he surveys at the office, but who feels inept and out of place at home with his family. No wonder he comes home from work so late every day.

The purpose of this book is not to make you a busier Christian, but to help you live a balanced, healthy Christian life.

The Not-Enough-Time Heresy

However we spend the hours in our day, each of us, rich and poor, young and old, vigorous and infirm, gets the same number of them. We can't stockpile them to use later. We're forced to live time as we receive it, sixty seconds for every minute, sixty minutes for every hour. Once lived, we can never retrieve those hours and live them again.

If we say that we don't have enough time, we're saying that God didn't give us enough. We're implying that his gift is inadequate and, further, that his plan for us must be wrong or that he intends to frustrate and thwart us.

What if we begin with the opposite assumption? Can you embrace the notion that your loving God, who desires what is good for you, has given you exactly as much time as you need? Then the challenge becomes not trying to find more time or lamenting its lack, but finding and conforming to the natural rhythms of your day and getting into harmony with God's plan for you. Time management becomes a way of seeking right living. That is precisely the purpose of this book: not to make you a busier Christian but to help you live a balanced, healthy Christian life.

As always, if we want to figure out how to live right, we must turn to prayer and to God's word, revealed in Sacred Scripture.

Biblical Principles of Time Stewardship

We can find dozens of Bible passages devoted to living daily life in harmony with God, but most of these deal with money, possessions, and "talents," and very few with time. The ones that do touch on time make it clear that we are to be aware of the passage of time and of the limits on our time on earth: "So teach us to count our days that we may gain a wise heart" (Ps 90:12).

We ask God to turn us away from lives of self-centered independence and toward greater maturity and spiritual dependence on God, the source of life.

"Man looks to his comforts, pleasures, pursuits, accomplishments, and wealth to find meaning, significance, satisfaction, and security in and with this life," the Bible.org Web site notes in an essay titled, "The Stewardship of Time: Multiplying the Life Through Redeeming the Time." "But one of the great messages of the Bible is such can only be found in God." Perhaps this is at the heart of Jesus' warning that it is easier for a camel to pass through the eye of a needle than for a rich person to get to heaven (cf. Mt 19:24 and Mk 10:25). The rich have so many distractions and so much more to lose.

America's storyteller, Garrison Keillor, posits that folks who live in places that provide harsh winters, like his beloved Norwegian bachelor farmers of Minnesota, have an easier time waging war against fleshly desires than do folks who bask in the eternal sunshine of California, Hawaii, or Florida. But we folks in the upper Midwest ice belt have plenty of other challenges to our virtue. Whether in Nome, Alaska, or Boca Raton, Florida, we are called to live godly lives, embracing good and shunning evil. "Be careful then how you live, not as unwise people but as wise, making the most of the time, because the days are evil. So do not be foolish, but understand what the will of God is" (Eph 5:15–17).

In his first letter, Peter lays out the principles clearly. First we must grasp that, as Christians, we are exiles from paradise, aliens on this earth (see 1 Pet 2:11). We know that we live in an evil age, a time of darkness. We are here to love and serve the Lord, to be ambassadors for Christ (see 1 Pet 3:15).

Finally, despite the evilness of the age and our status as aliens, Peter tells us: "But rejoice insofar as you are sharing Christ's sufferings, so that you may also be glad and shout for joy when his glory is revealed" (1 Pet 4:13).

Not feeling like much of an ambassador for Christ? No time to rejoice? Let's make time, first by taking stock of how well we're already managing our time. Then, in Part 2, we'll explore specific ways to manage it better.

CHAPTER 3

Do You Really Need to Manage Time?

> [I]t is now the moment for you to wake from sleep. For salvation is nearer to us now than when we became believers; the night is far gone, the day is near. (Rom 13:11–12)

It's more than a little ironic. We race from task to task, driven by a sense of urgency and the habit of hurry, and yet we act as if we had all the time in the world to tell our loved ones how much they mean to us, to mend a rift in a friendship, or to take the kids fishing.

Seasons fly by, and we never quite get around to taking in a ballgame or planting the garden or studying Swahili or reading Shakespeare. Like the Brooklyn Dodgers of old, our motto seems to be, "Wait'll next year."

The words of the psalmist should give us pause:

> LORD, let me know my end, and what is the measure of
>   my days;
> let me know how fleeting my life is.
> You have made my days a few handbreaths,
>   and my lifetime is as nothing in your sight.
> Surely everyone stands as a mere breath.
>   Surely everyone goes about like a shadow.
> Surely for nothing they are in turmoil;
>   They heap up, and do not know who will gather.
> (Ps 39:4–6)

Today, in Your Sight, the Prophecy Is Fulfilled

Imagine you were in the temple on that Sabbath morning when Jesus read the words of the prophet Isaiah from the holy scrolls and then told the assembly that the prophecy had been fulfilled, that the Messiah they had longed for was sitting right in front of them.

Would you have believed and, believing, rushed to embrace him? Or would you have doubted, scoffed, or even written Jesus off as a raving lunatic? Perhaps you might have been offended, even outraged. When the serviced ended and it was time to go home, what would you have done differently from what you had done on any other Sabbath?

What do we do now, 2,000 years later? Christ has told us that the kingdom is at hand. No more waiting for the Messiah! We have our Messiah, now and forever.

"Be careful then how you live," Paul cautions in Ephesians 5:15–16, "not as unwise people but as wise, making the most of the time." For "making the most of," Paul uses a form of the Greek verb *exagoraz*, which carries the sense of redeeming or freeing our time.

> [L]et us then lay aside the works of darkness and put on the armor of light; let us live honorably as in the day, not in reveling and drunkenness, not in debauchery and licentiousness, not in quarrelling and jealousy. Instead, put on the Lord Jesus Christ, and make no provision for the flesh, to gratify its desires. (Rom 13:12–13)
>
> So let us not grow weary in doing what is right, for we will reap at harvest time, if we do not give up. So then, whenever we have an opportunity, let us work for the good of all, and especially for those of the family of faith. (Gal 6:9–10)

We are to love and serve God and our fellows. We are to love our neighbor as our very selves. We are to tell folks about

Jesus, free the captives, feed the hungry, clothe the naked. We are to give to the one who asks, walk the second mile, as well as shed our coats and our shirts for those in need. And we are to do it now.

"Not everyone who says to me, 'Lord, Lord,' will enter into the kingdom of heaven," Jesus tells us in Matthew 7:21, "but only the one who does the will of my Father in heaven."

But to do any of that and still continue to function in all the roles God has given us—father, mother, homemaker, wage earner, student, teacher, and all the rest—takes conscious effort. As we know all too well, like that picnic in the park we keep intending to have "one of these nice, sunny Sunday afternoons real soon," we'll do none of these good works until and unless we make time for them. And to do that, we need to learn to manage our time effectively and live our lives intentionally.

How do you decide how to allocate the 1,440 minutes God gives to each of us every day? By what criteria do you make your time-management decisions? If you don't think about that, someone else will set the agenda for you. Every emergency, real or perceived, every desire or even whim of the dominant people in your life, will determine what you do. You may simply heed the call that is the loudest and most persistent—not the one that has the true claim on your time.

You may never hear the still, small voice of God calling to you.

The Biblical Case for Planning

Remember those foolish virgins (bridesmaids in some translations), the five who took their lamps to meet the bridegroom but failed to bring extra oil for those lamps? When their wicks burned low, they pleaded with the five well-prepared vigil-keepers to give them oil. A lesson in sharing? Not this time. The other five kept their oil, to make sure they wouldn't run out themselves and be plunged into darkness. The unprepared five sped off to town (to an all-night lamp oil shop?) to replenish their supplies. But the bridegroom arrived while they were gone and went into the wedding banquet with the five prepared women, shutting the door behind them.

> Later the other bridesmaids came also, saying, "Lord, lord, open to us." But he replied, "Truly I tell you, I do not know you." Keep awake therefore, for you know neither the day nor the hour. (Mt 25:11–13)

The Boy Scouts have it right: Be prepared.

> Blessed are those slaves whom the master finds alert when he comes; truly I tell you, he will fasten his belt and have them sit down to eat, and he will come and serve them. (Lk 12:37)

"'You also must be ready,'" Jesus concludes, "for the Son of Man is coming at an unexpected hour'" (Lk 12:40).

Later, in Luke 14:28 and following, Jesus offers us two more paragons of planning. The architect must work out the cost before building the tower, lest he run short of funds and materials, abandon the project before it's finished, and suffer ridicule. The king must calculate whether his 10,000 men can hold off the advancing army of twice that number. If not, the wise king will offer peace terms rather than fight.

But not all advance planning seems to work out well, as is the case with the rich farmer who enjoys a year of bumper crops in Luke 12:16 and following. He decides to pull down his barns and build bigger ones to hold all the grain, so he can kick back and relax for the rest of his life. "But God said to him, 'You fool! This very night your life is being demanded of you. And the things you have prepared, whose will they be?' So it is with those who store up treasures for themselves but are not rich toward God" (Lk 12:20–21).

So we are to plan ahead, but not to assure ourselves of treasure on earth. Jesus tells us to be like the lilies of the field and the birds of the sky, trusting in God to provide for us. We are to lay up for ourselves treasures in heaven, for "where your treasure is, there your heart will be also" (Mt 6:21).

Now is the fitting and proper time, the *kairos* time. We must redeem our time and our lives now, not later. But laying up that treasure in heaven—through prayer and worship and Scripture study, and through feeding the hungry and clothing the poor—requires time. If you're having trouble finding that time, you need to apply wise time management.

Taking Stock

Are you putting your time where your values are? How well are you managing *chronos* time, with the goal of preparing yourself to live in *kairos* time?

Two prominent researchers into how we spend our time disagree about how much or how little "free time" we have. In her 1991 bestseller, *The Overworked American*, Juliet B. Schor argues that, as our work week and the prevalence of the two-income family have expanded, leisure time has shrunk, trapping us in an "insidious cycle of work and spend." But researcher John P. Robinson, head of the American's Use of Time Project at the University of Maryland's Survey Research Center, asserts that our "perception of a time crunch appears to have gone up in the period of time where free time has increased."

More leisure but less time. They can't both be right, can they?

One reason for the seeming disparity, Robinson says, is that we spend, on average, almost 40 percent of our leisure time watching television, but somehow we don't seem to think of that time as "free."

A two-year Gallup Poll found that we spend 26 to 34 percent of our leisure time watching the tube (the amount depends on the day of the week, with Thursday being the peak television viewing day). Reading and socializing vie for a very distant second place, with well under 10 percent each.

Whether or not these numbers surprise or concern you, they aren't nearly as important as *your* numbers, the way you're spending your precious time. It might be worth keeping track of how you use your time for a couple of weeks, so you can have a rough starting point before you begin making changes.

In the workbook written to accompany this text, you will find a simple system for categorizing and cataloging your time over a two-week period. If you'd rather devise your own system, that's fine, too. However you chart it, you may find you have more flexibility in your schedule than you thought. You may discover opportunities to make meaningful decisions about how you spend your time.

Whatever your introspection reveals about you, you'll probably uncover some fundamental time-management challenges.

The TTC and the CCC Extremes

Perhaps you'll find yourself at the far end of the neatness/punctuality spectrum, a Tremendously Tidy Catholic (TTC) who keeps a neat office and a tight schedule. If that's you, your motto might be, "A place for everything and everything in its place," with color-coded folders and tabs to chart the territory. For you, being early is being on time, and being late is inexcusable.

And that's where your troubles may begin. What you can't tolerate in yourself you might find hard to excuse in others. If so, you may waste a lot of time and psychic energy waiting and fuming. You may also have a hard time abandoning your schedule, even just a little, to deal with the unforeseen in your life. With discipline can come rigidity.

The folks most likely to drive the TTC nuts fall into the CCC (Chronically Cluttered Catholic) category. If this is your song, your refrain may be, "A place for everything, and everything all over the place." You find yourself telling your TTC colleagues, "Sure, my office is messy, but I know exactly where everything is." For you, a schedule is a suggestion. Life happens, and somehow you always get off track. You fly by an estimated time of arrival, and your on-time record is no better than that of most airlines.

You probably fall somewhere in between these opposite ends of the space/time continuum, and you no doubt exhibit some of the characteristics of each. Appraise yourself honestly and decide what's working for you and what isn't (Can you *really* find everything without having to tear through stacks of clutter?) and set about changing the things that aren't.

That will be the goal of the next section of this book.

Part 2

How to Control Chronos Time

CHAPTER 4

10 Truths, 10 Tips, and the Fundamental Law of Time Management

TRUTH 1: Time management isn't always about a lack of time.

TIP 1: Face the tasks you've been avoiding by being "too busy." In particular, stop wasting time on the "merely urgent" and make time for the "important but not urgent."

As you begin the work of effectively managing the precious time God gives you each day, remove "I don't have enough time" and "I'm too busy" from the discussion. You have as much time as you're ever going to have and as much as you're ever going to need.

Often "I don't have enough time" and similar laments mask a deeper problem, an aversion to the task that needs doing. You always know what you should be doing, just as you always know what the right and good thing to do is in any given situation. God has planted that knowledge deep within each of us. The trick is to listen and to act, despite contrary feelings.

TRUTH 2: Day-planners and to-do lists make good servants but lousy masters.

TIP 2:　Don't overload the list.

You must control your list of things to do; you mustn't let the list control you. Keep the list flexible. Consider it a map, a guide. Mark your desired destination for the day, but be aware that you might not get that far or that God may have a different destination in mind for you.

If you don't accomplish everything on the list, that's why God made tomorrow. Praise him and thank him for the day you've had, for the work you've been able to accomplish, for any good you might have done, for anyone whose burden you may have eased along the way. Go to sleep.

TRUTH 3:　You will never "find" time.

TIP 3:　You must "make" time for whatever you want and need to do.

Time isn't missing. It's right here. You just don't notice because you live in time the way a fish lives in water. You have time—which is to say life—in abundance because God gave it to you. You didn't earn or deserve it. There's no way you could. It's God's gift, freely given in love.

TRUTH 4:　Other people will make you wait.

TIP 4:　Turn the wait into a rest.

Waiting is part of the price you pay for living in society and depending on other people. It's stressful—but living alone could be even more stressful. You'll wait in line, wait in traffic, wait for the babysitter, wait for the meeting to start, wait for the phone to ring and the mail to run. Accept it.

Accept, too, that you'll make other people wait, too. You won't do it on purpose. You won't mean to inconvenience anyone. You'll just be trying to live your life. Every time you find yourself in a traffic jam, remember, you're part of the jam.

Forgive all those folks who are making your life inconvenient and pray they'll forgive you.

TRUTH 5:   Multitasking can be counterproductive.

TIP 5:   Do one thing at a time.

Multitasking can be bad for your physical, mental, and spiritual well-being. You can't really do two things at once—not well, anyway—especially if they require any sort of mental attention. When you split your attention, you diminish it, and the two tasks compete.

You no doubt practice serial multitasking every day. You have to in order to get anything (let alone everything) done. You get interrupted, setting one task aside and taking up another, often in a split second, sometimes without even being aware you're doing it. But to be effective, you must shift your full attention to the new task until it's time to return to the original job.

When folks advise you to "live in the now," they're really telling you to focus your attention completely on what you're doing and who you're with. Do what you're doing, see what you're seeing, hear what you're hearing. Don't replay what came before or anticipate what comes next.

TRUTH 6:   Work expands to fill available time.

TIP 6:   When you're finished, move on.

If you don't set a time limit (or have one set for you), a task is likely to eat up as much time as you let it. You can always do a little more or do it a little better. You must set reasonable limits. Create a schedule and stick to it.

The more you do a task, the better you'll learn to make an accurate estimate of how long it should take (and how many interruptions and waits you're likely to encounter) the next time you do the same or a similar task.

TRUTH 7:   Not only *can* you schedule creativity; you *have to* schedule creativity.

TIP 7:   Make a date with your muse—and then keep that date.

Thinking creatively sometimes involves being struck by inspiration. Those wonderful "ah-ha!" moments sometimes hit you, life's little eurekas, when a knotty problem miraculously unravels, the fog clears, the solution reveals itself. Embrace these breakthroughs and thank God for them. But don't rely on them.

That sort of subconscious lightning only strikes when you've prepared for it consciously. Unless you've been writing music and playing the guitar for many years, the way Paul Stookey had, for example, you're not likely to wake up one morning with the words and tune for the beautiful and haunting "Wedding Song" playing in you. Stookey did—after trying for weeks to write a song for his best friend Peter Yarrow's wedding. (Along with Mary Travers, they are the famous folk trio, Peter, Paul, and Mary.) After the wedding, Yarrow persuaded his friend to share the song with the rest of us.

No less a creative thinker than Louis Pasteur noted, "Chance favors the prepared mind." The trouble is, we're often so busy, overscheduled, and pressured that we don't pay attention to our inspirations. Creativity becomes an interruption or an inconvenience.

When lightning doesn't strike—and you need to come up with a solution right now anyway—you can be creative on a deadline. It isn't fun. It might even be painful. But you can do it. You might feel that your solution falls short, but that is an illusion. You can't judge the worth of your creation right after you fashion it. (That's like asking a mother to be objective about her newborn baby.)

Creativity sometimes takes time. It may require quiet, even solitude (or as close to quiet and solitude as you can manage). That means you have to prepare a time and a place for creative thinking. Schedule creative thinking and then honor that appointment as much as you would a trip to the dentist or a meeting with the boss.

TRUTH 8:   Every workplace contains at least one
             time/energy "black hole."

TIP 8:   To keep your energy level high, avoid whiners and
           complainers.

Some folks just seem to have a bad attitude. They get up on the wrong side of life every morning, and all day long they sing the "ain't-it-awful" blues. There's no problem so simple they can't complicate it, no potential solution so good they can't shoot it down.

"It'll never work," they assure you. "We've never done it that way before."

When nothing in particular challenges them, they complain about life in general, about "them" and how "they" are making things difficult.

Pray for these negative people. Then make sure you don't become one of them. Stay away from whiners and complainers as much as you can.

TRUTH 9:   Mama was right. You really *do* work and feel
             better when you're well rested.

TIP 9:   Rest when you're weary.

Maybe all you really need to work more efficiently is a good nap. In general, we're not sleeping as much as we used to. A few decades back the average American got eight hours of sleep a night, but now we average only six to six and a half. And in our culture, we don't take a siesta. We think naps are for babies and old folks.

That's a shame, because a lot of us may be spending the afternoon fighting off sleep and trying to keep alert with sugar and caffeine when all we really need is a twenty-minute nap. If you can't sit in a quiet room for five minutes without nodding off, you're sleep-deprived. If so, make getting more sleep one of your top time-management priorities.

TRUTH 10: By the time you need a vacation, it's too late to take one.

TIP 10: Take four vacations every day.

That's not a typographical error. You need four vacations *every working day*. Many of us labor all year for a two- or three-week vacation (if we're lucky). More and more of us don't even take a vacation at all. We're too busy, too work-addicted, too convinced that the world will crumble if we aren't on the job to run things.

But we need our vacations—we need them for physical, mental, and spiritual health. If you're fortunate enough to have a job that provides for a block of vacation time, you would be well advised to take and embrace it!

The yearly vacation isn't enough. We need our weekends, too (whether it comes at the traditional end of the week or not). "Thank God it's Friday" has become a rallying cry in our culture. But here again, more and more of us are letting work encroach on our days off, taking the work with us wherever we go.

But even if you take a refreshing vacation every year and reserve every weekend for play and rest, it still may not be enough. By the time you finally battle your way to Friday afternoon, you may be so knotted up with accumulated stress, so addicted to caffeine and adrenaline, so engrained in the habit of hurry, that you can't relax, can't enjoy your recreation, or can't fall asleep at night even though you're exhausted.

That's why you need to take four short "vacations" every day, to break the stress cycle and relax mind and body. (We'll explore seven specific "sanctifying sanity breaks" in chapter 11.)

The Fundamental Law of Time Management

When you make time for a task,
you don't actually create more time.
You take it from something else.

Now it's up to you. You can memorize these ten tips, have them bronzed and laminated, inscribe them on plaques, and hang them around your home and office. But unless you start actually living them, they won't do you a bit of good. The next eleven chapters of this book are full of specific ways to put these tips into practice.

Ready to get started?

Chapter 5

Moment Management

Now I invite you to take a close look at your daily life, examining it moment by moment. Specifically, you will uncover the little decisions that go into a day in your life. The point will be to reclaim some of those decisions that you may now be making passively, by default.

If you're like most of us, you make lots of daily decisions without even thinking about them. The day's choices may even begin the night before; perhaps you lay out the clothes you'll wear. Some folks draft a to-do list for the coming day. Last thing before retiring, perhaps you set an alarm clock, which means you've decided when you must get up the next day.

Suppose that when that alarm goes off, let's say at 6:30, you decide to hit the snooze alarm and catch five more minutes of sleep. (You might in fact "decide" to do this every day, perhaps more than once per morning.) Do you have time for a shower? If so, will you wash your hair? Which brand of shampoo? Will you use a conditioner, too?

You make these sorts of decisions by rote, and that's good. If you spent time and psychic energy deciding what kind of toothpaste to use and whether to start brushing upper left or lower right, you'd never get anywhere.

But some of these choices deserve and even require review from time to time, to make sure you're being a wise steward of your time. For example, perhaps you've set the alarm for 6:30 every working day for decades. If that works for you, there's no need to change. But you could set it for thirty minutes earlier to accommodate some new activity you want to introduce into your life or to combat chronic lateness at work. Or you could set it for thirty minutes later, hoping the extra sleep will more than compensate for the need to move faster when you do get up. You could even completely skip setting the alarm, trusting habit to get you up or leaving it to "fate" to rouse you on time. ("If you want me to go to work tomorrow, Lord, be sure to wake me up on time. If you don't, I'll take it as a sign that you want me to stay home.")

I'm not saying you ever *would* or *should* do any of these things. I'm just saying you could. You always have a choice. The consequences of some options may be so awful, even unthinkable, that you don't recognize them as options at all, but the options still remain. You could withhold 40 percent of your income taxes this year, for example, as many do, to protest the government's foreign policy. If you did, you might go to jail, a rather dire consequence, but it's still an option, and some people exercise it.

If you do feel the need to revisit some of your daily life choices, use the simple 3R method: read the situation, reflect on your choices, and respond with a decision. Then reject the fourth R—remorse. Don't second-guess yourself or keep remaking the decision for hours.

Let's examine the anatomy of a relatively simple but routine-altering decision. Let's suppose you've been trying to make regular exercise part of your daily regimen. You pledge to begin riding your bike to work instead of driving. Great idea! You'll get great exercise, save money, and help preserve the environment while reducing our country's dependence on foreign oil.

But when you get up in the morning, it looks as if it might rain, and your knee aches, and you figure maybe this wouldn't be such a good day to start biking to work after all. Ride the bike or drive the car? You have to make a decision.

Do you have other options? Of course. You always do.

○ You could take the bus. You wouldn't get the exercise, but you would save some money while doing something to fight climate change by not driving your car. On the down side, you'd have to wait outside at the bus stop, and you'd have to walk three blocks from the stop downtown to your office. You still have to consider the possibility of rain.

○ You could walk to work. You'd get exercise and fresh air, save money, be a friend of the earth—but you'd have to leave for work a lot earlier, and you still might get rained on. Oh, and there's that dicey knee to consider.

○ Take a cab? Hire a limo? Hitchhike? (Does anybody do that anymore?) Stay home? See if you can get a ride with a neighbor who drives downtown about the same time you do every day?

Without too much effort, you can easily swamp yourself in possibilities.

The Art of Making a Decision and Sticking to It

What you decide on any given day may not be as important as *that* you decide, quickly and decisively. Difficulty making decisions may be part of your time-management problem, perhaps even your biggest challenge. You may spend too much time and psychic energy weighing options. Perhaps you've become an expert at talking yourself out of all the options. Since no choice is ideal, none is acceptable. Now what?

Perhaps something deeper underlies your need to pick apart every potential option. You might be afraid of making a mistake, of doing it wrong, of looking foolish.

The Three Primary Fears that Keep Us from Making a Decision

First Source of Fear: *Uncertainty*

"Are you *sure?*"

These three seemingly innocent little words can cripple your ability to make a decision.

Others may seem much more confident than you, but they probably aren't. You only see their actions and outward demeanor. You're not there when worry keeps them awake at night; you can't see the doubt that may fester in their minds, just as it does in yours. But you're acutely aware of your own fears.

Second Source of Fear: *Ignorance*

"If I had only known."

We all know the feeling. Sometimes we get the information and insight we need much too late to use it. That's frustrating. It may even be enraging. Any embarrassment and anger you feel can help you later if it teaches you something about your decision-making that can help you make a better decision next time.

But these feelings can also work against you if you allow them to render you unwilling or even unable to act decisively the next time you face a similar choice. You fear looking like a chump—again—because you didn't know everything. And that fear can freeze you.

Third Source of Fear: *Failure*

"Play to win," coaches urge.

A fundamental truth lies behind this obvious aphorism. If you play to avoid losing, you'll be stiff and cautious. It's the difference between trying to catch a ball and trying to avoid dropping it. The first mind-set is positive and encourages aggressive effort; the second is negative and promotes hesitation.

Often we're taught to avoid failure rather than seek success. Instead of learning how to read, write, and do math confidently, for example, our schooling may teach us to avoid mistakes while trying to read and write, add and subtract. An activity that should bring us joy becomes an agony, something to dread.

I remember sitting in my "magpie" reading group, struggling to work out Dick and Jane's relationships with Mom, Dad, Spot, and Puff. When the teacher called on me to read aloud, I was so scared, I could barely see the page. When I inevitably stumbled and made a mistake, the other kids laughed. (They were as nervous as I was, and laughter can relieve tension.) I felt like a fool. The teacher corrected me, and I stumbled on, trying to avoid stepping on the next land mine.

Learning to write should be a joyful process of discovering your voice and learning your own mind. Instead, it can turn into a constant struggle to avoid having misspelled words circled and grammar errors underlined in red. Instead of helping you learn how numbers work, arithmetic can become a war to get the right answers and avoid the wrong ones, even if we don't understand what we're doing or why we're doing it. It's easy to see how these fears can carry over into other facets of life. It would be a miracle if they didn't.

The Three Primary Keys to Combating These Fears

1. You don't have to be sure.

When John F. Kennedy defeated Richard Nixon for president in 1960, he received just 49.7 percent of the popular vote, with 49.6 going to Nixon. That means the country was 49.7 percent "sure" it would rather have Kennedy than Nixon lead it. Did Kennedy's election make a difference for the country and the world? Of course it did.

Sometimes you can only be 49.7 percent "certain" of your decision. But you have to let that be enough for you to act.

2. *You don't have to know everything.*

You can't, no matter how much you study.

Before you let your fear of not having all the information you need paralyze you, remember than hindsight is always a lot clearer than the view you had before you made your decision. You'll always get information and feedback after the fact.

If you insist on trying to gather all the information and anticipating all the potential outcomes before you act, you never will. Accept this as inevitable. You don't have to know it all, because you can't. You don't have to be sure, because you won't be. And best of all—

3. *You don't even have to be right.*

Nobody is, not 100 percent of the time.

Sometimes there isn't even a clear "right" or "wrong." There's only this way and the other way—and then let's see how things turn out.

You don't have to be right, but you do have to decide—and then stick to your decision, not wasting time or energy by second-guessing yourself. In our hypothetical example about commuting to work, suppose you bet on rain and took the car instead of biking to work. The sun came out just as you nosed the car into the parking ramp downtown. It turned into a beautiful spring day, perfect for a bike ride. You were wrong. You blew it.

So what?

It wouldn't be the first time you guessed wrong on the weather, and it won't be the last. You haven't lost anything irreplaceable, and tomorrow is another day and another decision. Maybe God had some reason to want you to have the car downtown that day. Suppose you had taken the bike and gotten rained on? You arrived at work soaking wet and plenty mad. That's embarrassing and inconvenient, to say the least. But you wouldn't have taken the chance on rain if you had a big client meeting that morning, right? You would have factored that into the equation. You'll dry out. You won't shrink, and your colors won't run. This, too, shall pass.

Wrong choices either make a significant difference or they don't. If the outcome doesn't matter all that much, even if, with that wonderful clarity of hindsight, you now see that another choice would have been better, just let it go. Banish regrets and second-guessing.

If your decision does matter, admit your mistake, accept the blame and the consequences, and make it right any way you can. Learn from your mistake and move on.

And know this: no matter how dire things may look at the moment, most decisions, even some of the large ones, fall into the first category. Most of the time, you really can't make a serious mistake. The only mistake you really make is not making a decision.

Remember Robert Frost's poem in which he writes, "I took the (road) less traveled by, and that has made all the difference"? Some decisions are huge. The decision to get married (or not, or not yet, or to someone else), to move from the country to the city (or the city to the country, or from one town to another), to take the job (or another job, or another career, or to try out the beachcomber lifestyle) all can have huge consequences. But you can't see most of those long-term outcomes until you make the decision and start to live it.

Sometimes the unintended consequences, good or bad, don't become evident for years.

Whatever decision you make, your life will contain suffering and struggle. No decision could render you immune from that. But your life will also include joy, growth, and learning, "the thrill of victory," as the late Jim McKay used to say at the beginning of every edition of *ABC's Wide World of Sports*, along with "the agony of defeat."

Viewed in this way, no decision is ever truly a mistake.

Don't Just Make the Call: Sell It!

Who knows more about making difficult decisions under intense pressure than a sports official?

If you want advice on decision making, listen to an umpire or referee. Better still, listen to Barry Mano, publisher of *Referee* magazine and founder of the National Association of Sports Officials. Mano says that making the right call is really all about preparation: knowing the rules, being in position to make the call, and hustling as hard as—and sometimes even harder than—the players.

But then he adds something I never would have thought of. You don't just *make* the call, he stresses. You also have to *sell* the call. Make your call clearly and emphatically, so that no one can misunderstand it or doubt your authority to make it. You're not claiming infallibility; you're simply asserting your right and responsibility to make the decision and making it clear that this is the decision you've made.

Then stick to it. Sports officials sometimes face mobs of howling fans. Managers and coaches argue with vehemence. The criticism and disapproval you face may be considerably more subtle but no less intimidating.

Does that mean you'll never make a mistake? Of course not. It doesn't even mean you won't be tempted to second-guess yourself, especially in light of strong opinion to the contrary. It does mean you'll make timely decisions instead of letting doubt and anxiety paralyze you. If you later realize you made the wrong call, admit it, make it right if you can, and get on with it.

The Most Powerful Word in the World

Some of the most important decisions you'll make each day arise when others make demands on your time. For these cases, you need to learn to unleash the most empowering word you'll ever utter, one that many two-year-olds use nearly to the exclusion of all others.

That word is "no."

It's one of the hardest words for some adults to say in response to a request for help. And that isn't necessarily because they're so incredibly nice. At least four other reasons may cause you to choke on the word "no," so that it comes out as "Sure. Be glad to."

Reason 1: Looking for love in some of the wrong places

We try to earn the gratitude and approval—maybe even the respect—of others when we shoulder their burdens. We all want to be accepted, and we may fear, deep down, that if we don't do the extra work, others will have no use for us.

Reason 2: Bearing guilt

Of course it's for a good cause. And they certainly wouldn't have asked unless they really needed your help. And of course you'll be letting them down if you don't say yes. But sometimes you still have to say no.

Reason 3: Believing the myth of indispensability

Rather than kindness, your efforts may in part be motivated by a subtle form of arrogance. You take the extra job because you feel you're the only one who can do it well. "If you want something done right," the old saw goes, "do it yourself."

Reason 4: Fearing expendability

This is the flip side of reason 3. You may feel that if you don't do the job, someone else will step in and do it just as well or better than you could have. Folks may start realizing that they really don't need you at all.

Although reasons 3 and 4 seem to be mutually exclusive, it's quite possible to feel both ways at the same time!

How to Say No

Sometimes you have to say no, even to a legitimate request to aid a good cause. Time given to this new task must come from someplace else—perhaps from sleep, family time, or prayer. You won't be given new time, and you can't create it.

If you want to take on the new task, decide what, if anything, you're willing to trade for the new job. In simple terms, the question is, "If I start doing this, what will I stop doing?" If the answer is "nothing," then you need to say no. Here's how to say it.

1. Stifle the automatic yes.

For some of us, "I'll be glad to" is a reflex, as natural as sneezing. That reflex gets us in big trouble. As tough as it is to say no when asked, it's much harder to say it later, after you've already agreed to do something.

So the first step in saying no is to take a breath and to say nothing.

2. Buy time.

Unless you're already quite certain of your decision, one way or the other, take time to think about it and consult with those in your life who will be affected. "Let me get back to you tomorrow" is a reasonable—and often necessary—response.

3. If the answer is no, say no.

Say it gracefully and gratefully ("I'm flattered that you asked me. Thanks for thinking of me.") But *say* it. Then stop talking.

4. You don't have to give a reason.

When we do work up the gumption to decline a request for our time, we almost invariably follow the no with a because. We shouldn't.

You don't want to be rude, and of course you want folks to see the wisdom and even the rightness of your decision, so you may try to prove it:

- ○ "I'm just too busy."
- ○ "I've got Cub Scouts that night."
- ○ "I don't think I'd do a very good job."

Your ardent suitor will counter every argument.

- ○ "I know you're busy, but you know what they say: 'Ask a busy person.' And it really won't take much time."

Now what? If you continue to argue, you're implying that you think your petitioner is lying about the amount of time involved.

- ○ "We can change the meeting night to accommodate your schedule."

Trapped again. If you don't surrender, you'll have been found out offering a bogus excuse.

⭘ "With your brains and organizational skills, you're perfect for the job!"

Nah, I'm really an idiot. Trust me.

Now you've got an argument, or at least a discussion. What if you run out of reasons and lose the debate? You either have to acquiesce or tacitly admit that you really don't have a good reason for declining. Both of you will be much more upset that you would have been.

Don't give a reason. Just say no.

The Three Little Words That Can Eat Up Your Time

We've been discussing straightforward requests for your time, things like:

⭘ "Would you be willing to serve on the parish council?"

⭘ "Could you coach the sixth-grade soccer team this season?"

⭘ "I'm moving out of my apartment Saturday. Could you help me?"

The ambiguous request for time can be even more difficult to deal with, things like, "Are you busy?" or the even more insidious "Got a minute?"

You're a conscientious and caring human being, so you stifle the sarcastic or confrontational response ("I've got the same number of minutes you do! Why do you ask?"). Instead, you respond with something like, "Sure. What can I do for you?"

You've just signed a blank check, to be drawn on your time rather than your bank account. Now the caller gets to fill in the amount. Sign enough of these checks, and you'll find your time account overdrawn at the end of the day.

This is one case where you need to answer a question with a question. To decide whether to talk now, talk later, or not talk at all, you need two crucial bits of information not contained in the vague salvo, "Got a minute?":

1. Exactly how many of those minutes do you need?
2. How would we be spending those minutes?

If you don't ask, you're not managing your time effectively.

You can find lots of nice ways to ask. For example, "How may I help you?" focuses on the other person's needs while still providing the information you need. "What would you like to talk about?" is blunter but probably fine in most contexts.

You could buy a little time by saying something like, "Could I get back to you in half an hour? I'm right in the middle of something." You've still signed a promissory note, though, without knowing the amount due.

It's also quite appropriate to set your own time limit. "I've only got five minutes right now. If you need more time, it will have to wait."

The same sort of strategy applies when you respond to the assertion that "We need to schedule a meeting." Assert your right to ask questions and decide based on the answers you get before whipping out your day planner and starting to look for an open block of time to commit. You need to know:

○ The subject of the meeting.

○ The reason why it requires a meeting (instead of a brief conversation right then, for example, or a group email).

○ The reason you need to attend such a meeting.

As you hone your own effective and tactful responses, you'll also figure out good ways to ask for someone else's time, rather than being guilty of the same "Got a minute?" rudeness: "I need about five minutes of your time to discuss the Aaron's project with you. Is this a good time?"

This chapter may seem overly negative; we *are* discussing ways to say no, after all. But by saying no to one request, you can then say yes to spending that time on the people and activities most important to you.

Who really deserves your time? Is it the person who asks for it first or is the loudest and most persistent in asking? Are there silent ones in your life who need and deserve more attention from you than they're getting? By taking from one, you have more to give to the other.

We've gotten one big obstacle out of the way. The next chapter deals with more ways to free up time by eliminating tasks you shouldn't be doing.

CHAPTER 6

Eliminating Time Wasters

How many of your daily tasks do you perform simply because you've always performed them? You've got solid reasons for good habits like brushing and flossing, and you can easily justify taking the time to do them every day. But what about those tasks that have no value to you or to anyone else, the ones you do by rote simply because they've become part of your routine?

Many of these might fall into the "not urgent and not important" category. If working the morning crossword puzzle still brings you pleasure and satisfaction, and if your day affords you the time for it, then by all means go to it. But if it's no longer fun, if it has become just another chore to get through as rapidly as possible before going on to the next, it's time to drop it.

Other time eaters may seem urgent, but when you stop to think about them—and that's the whole point of this chapter—they really aren't important, let alone necessary. You do them because somebody tells you (or told you, perhaps long ago) to do them.

You'll learn to ferret out these time wasters by asking yourself some variation on the "Lakein Question," first proposed by Alan Lakein in his 1973 book, *How to Get Control of Your Time and Your Life*. My version goes like this:

Is this what I want or need to be doing right now?

Each element in the sentence is important: *I, want, need*, and *right now*.

Do you *want* or *need* to do it? Most of us do things every day that we don't want to do, but we know we need to, and we do them. But if you catch yourself at a task that you neither want nor need to do—one that isn't benefiting anyone—dump it. Get rid of busywork, activity for the sake of activity, and tasks you perform to avoid doing more important and difficult jobs.

Do you need to be doing it *right now?* More pressing tasks may be waiting for your attention—and weighing heavily on your subconscious mind. Decide on a time when you'll come back to the less important activity, and then tackle the more urgent chore.

Time management often isn't a matter of time at all. We "don't have time" for jobs we don't want to do. We put other, less important tasks ahead of them. When we stop evading and start rearranging our activities in their true order of priority, we're exercising real time management.

Take the pledge to root out busywork and work-avoidance work. You will likely free up time to do what you really want or need to be doing right now.

You may need to remind yourself often to ask yourself: *Is this what I want or need to be doing right now?* Some sort of tangible prompt, such as Post-it notes, can be helpful. You could even set an alarm to go off at certain intervals, perhaps every ninety minutes, and catch yourself in the midst of an activity.

If a task has become habitual—and such habits can become deeply engrained in the fabric of daily life—you may feel uneasy about dropping it. But as days and weeks pass, and life seems to go on without disastrous consequences—or any consequences at all—you'll begin to breathe easier and put the time you've reclaimed to better use.

In the meantime, you may want to put such chores on a "not-to-do list," as a reminder.

If the answer to *Is this what I want or need to be doing right now?* turns out to be yes and you do indeed want or need to be doing the activity right now, keep doing it. You'll have affirmed the rightness of your choice, and you'll feel a sense of control over your daily life that you may not have felt in years.

The "Let-George-Do-It" List

We need to examine one more vital word in my version of the Lakein Question: *I*. The job may need doing. It may even need doing right now. But you may not be the one who should be doing it—even if you've been doing it for years. You may lack the expertise, ability, information, tools, or authority to do the job as well as someone else could. Perhaps if you are doing the job for which you're not well matched, other tasks that you could do best won't get done.

Once you determine that someone else should be doing a job that you're now doing, you have three tools to use to enlist someone else to do it instead.

1. Delegating

In my work at the University of Wisconsin in Madison, I'm blessed with two wonderful program assistants, Diane and Laura. These wonderful women answer phones, sort mail, design and fill out forms, and catch my idiotic mistakes. For example, I ask them to proofread the copy for my newsletter rather than doing it myself. They do a much better job than I would.

But I've had to learn to *let* them help me! My inclination has always been to do it myself (perhaps to save myself the embarrassment of having someone else see my errors). I first began delegating jobs to them by necessity—I simply could no longer keep up—and have learned to appreciate, trust, and treasure the work they do with me.

If you aren't blessed with folks like Diane and Laura, you still have two other options.

2. *Swapping*

A few years back, we had a program assistant in my department—since retired—who loved to fill out and file forms but dreaded having to answer the telephone. Another assistant, also now retired, hated the paperwork but loved handling phone inquiries; you could hear the pleasure in her voice when she did. Not surprisingly, the first assistant wasn't all that great at handling callers, while the second was invariably courteous, cheerful, and helpful on the phone, but made lots of errors on forms. Neither had the authority to delegate work to the other, but they could and did arrange a swap, with their supervisor's approval.

Some folks never even consider delegating or swapping. They wouldn't think of having someone else answer the phone, sort the mail, or proofread the software presentation—not because they can't get someone else to help, but because they won't let them. These folks need to learn to use the third tool:

3. *Letting go*

The "I'd rather do it myself" mentality may indicate a deep-seated belief that "no one else could possibly do the job as well as I can." It may also stem from insecurity, the fear that you won't be needed unless you do everything yourself.

Even if you do delegate a job to someone else, you may find yourself supervising the work so closely that you spend as much time on it as you would have had you just done it your-self—and you may be alienating a coworker in the process.

Steel yourself and hand the job over, with no bungee cord attached. Clearly state your expectations for what you want done and how you want it done. Then keep hands off, even if you see that the other person isn't doing it "right" (meaning "your way"). You'll save time, and your coworker won't have to put up with your fussing.

Do it now. Do it later. Do it never. Let someone else do it. Those are the decisions you make when you start asking yourself: *Is this what I want or need to be doing right now?*

The "Good Enough" Principle of Time Management

If it has to be perfect, you've got a problem.

I'm certainly not advocating shoddy work—but I suspect that's not an issue here. People who read time-management books tend to be extremely conscientious. The line between "conscientiousness" and "perfectionism" can be very fine, and perfectionists have a tough time ever finishing anything.

How good is "good enough"? It depends on who's going to see it and what they're going to do with it. Working figures for a preliminary budget don't need to be carried out to ten decimal places, and they don't need to be laser printed on glossy paper in four colors.

One of my favorite of Gary Larson's *Far Side* cartoons includes a dog, the dog's master, a lawn mower, and the myth of perfectionism. Here's the scene: The dog has just finished trying to mow the law with a push mower, as evidenced by a wavy path cut through the tall grass. The dog's master is standing on the stoop, glaring down at the dog. "You call that mowing the lawn!" he's shouting. "Bad dog! No biscuit!"

Okay, the dog didn't do the job perfectly. In fact, it was downright patchy. By human standards, he made a botch of things. But the irate master has overlooked two fundamental points. First, the dog has done the best he could. (It's tough to even reach the handle on that old push mower!) Second, and most importantly, *the dog mowed the lawn!* Lassie never mowed a lawn (or got Timmy out of a well, for that matter). Rin Tin Tin never mowed a lawn. Yukon King never even saw a lawn! A dog mowing a lawn is miraculous! Doesn't that dog deserve a biscuit for its heroic effort and for the partial, if imperfect, achievement? Don't you?

How the Bad Dog! No Biscuit! Mentality Defeats You

The all-or-nothing attitude will often get you nothing.

If a job has to be done perfectly or not at all, you're much less likely to attempt it in the first place. The penalty for "failure" is just too great, and failure is almost assured if you insist on measuring your performance against some impossibly high ideal.

In writers I call it the "Shakespeare Syndrome." I'll never be able to write as well as Shakespeare, the argument goes, so why bother writing at all? Because the world doesn't need another Shakespeare, I tell them. We've still got the works of the original. The world needs your best work, your vision, written your way. If you insist on perfection, your best work will never be good enough.

Why Practice Makes Pretty Darn Good

You will never attain the ideal form, because it's an illusion that exists only in your mind. But you can and will get better and better at what you do.

Practice won't make perfect—unless it's perfect practice, in which case you've already attained the goal before you start.

But as you gain experience, learn from previous efforts, master skills, gather feedback, and compare the results you get with the results you hoped for, you'll attain greater and greater mastery.

In the beginning, grant yourself permission to be rotten. Have the courage to embrace a radical new motto: "Anything worth doing is worth doing badly." Banish the notion of "mistake" from your thinking. You're not making mistakes; you're learning.

Do it now; judge it later. If creativity gets tangled up in judgment, criticism stifles performance every time.

Your evolution from cautious critic to dynamic producer will take time. You'll backslide into perfectionism often. Be gentle with yourself and keep learning. You'll free yourself to be more productive than in your wildest perfectionist dreams.

The same goes for gaining mastery over one of the fundamental tools of time management, the to-do list. We'll turn to that worthy topic in the next chapter.

CHAPTER 7

To Do or Not to Do

Taming the Day Planner

There's nothing new about the to-do list. We may have invented better (and certainly more complicated) devices, but the concept remains the same: list tasks that must be done and rank them in the order in which we should do them.

Alan Lakein spells out the uses and misuses of the to-do list in *How to Get Control of Your Time and Your Life*. We're to use the list, Lakein stresses, to get everything done, yes, but with the goal of living a happy, healthy, well-rounded life. Lakein has the wisdom to consider rest, recreation, and relationships as important components of that full life.

Subsequent iterations of the concept have taken us to a much less gentle place, where the idea becomes to cram as much work as humanly possible into a limited amount of time. That sort of approach leads some to create:

A To-Do List from Hell

You plan to start the day with ten minutes of exercise and a quick read of the *Wall Street Journal*. Breakfast will be a power bar and a travel mug of coffee for the seventeen-minute commute to work, during which you'll listen to a motivational self-help tape "compressed" (pauses taken out) so you can hear twenty-two minutes' worth of advice in only seventeen minutes. You'll of course check your messages on your cell phone as soon as you finish your power bar.

At work you've allotted time for voice mail and e-mail, the morning staff meeting, and ninety minutes to finish your fact-gathering for the quarterly report. You plan twenty minutes for lunch in the cafeteria—a nutritious salad with low-calorie dressing. In the afternoon you'll devote an hour to the regular monthly meeting of the Workplace Expectations Committee and two hours to writing the first third of that quarterly report, along with answering e-mail and handling phone calls.

You're allowing a full nineteen minutes for the drive home, because you plan to stop to pick up the dry cleaning you forgot on Friday.

That's the plan. Here's what really happens:

You can't drag yourself out of bed in time for the sit-ups and push-ups, and you have a tough time focusing on the newspaper. They've started road construction on your commuting route, and some unfortunate driver has had a fender bender, which causes a huge traffic snarl, during which you spill coffee on your new suit.

You arrive at work twenty-seven minutes behind schedule, tear through voice and e-mail, and rush to your staff meeting—which runs twenty-four minutes over because one of your coworkers won't stop babbling about copy machine jams and theft from the employee refrigerator. As a result, you only get in ten minutes on the report.

Lunch is a candy bar and a bag of chips from the vending machine downstairs. You eat at your desk while working on the report.

In the afternoon constant phone calls bombard you, and the committee meeting runs longer than planned. You put in twenty more minutes on the report before a crisis erupts in the Toledo office, and it takes you over an hour to quell it.

You finally break loose, tense and exhausted, the report barely begun, for the commute home—and promptly get stuck in traffic again. (The road construction! You forgot!) You neglect to pick up the dry cleaning and arrive home an hour late for dinner, head aching, shoulder muscles tied in knots.

Think I've been too rough on the poor schedule? You know better. I even allowed for someone else to make the dinner and didn't throw in any kids or pets for you to take care of.

Whatever the particulars of your day—whether you spend it at an office or a factory, at home or behind a cash register at the local big-box store—the fallacy of the overstuffed to-do list remains a constant. We plan for that perfect day—no traffic tie-ups, no interruptions, no emergencies. Then life happens. When's the last time you had a perfect day?

Let's get real. Let's plan so you run the list, instead of the list running you.

Ten Tips for Creating a Workable To-Do List

1. Don't put too much on it.

This is fundamental. Master this and everything else falls into place.

Be realistic about your expectations and your time estimates. Make a real-world list, not an itinerary for fantasyland. If you don't, you'll spend every day running late and running scared. You'll be too cranky, preoccupied, and exhausted to notice how much your efficiency drops.

If you jam the list, it will run you. Instead, you must run the list. Let it help you organize, keep on task, and get the important jobs done first.

2. *Leave some air in the list.*

In order to accomplish Number 1, you need to learn to do Number 2.

Overestimate the commute time, allowing for the car dawdling in the fast lane and the cautious driver who makes you miss the left-turn arrow. Factor in the wait before the meeting starts and the time wasted during the meeting.

The more often you do a task, the better able you'll be to estimate how long it will take you to do it well. Other people's experience won't help much here; we all work at different paces, and what's easy for one person is difficult for another.

3. *List probabilities, not imperatives.*

You're making a list of the tasks you need, want, and hope to accomplish. It's your blueprint and time budget, and it isn't binding on anyone else in the universe. Think of it as a wish list.

What happens when you don't get everything on the list done? As a boyhood friend of mine used to say, "That's why God invented mañana."

Suppose you get sick and miss a whole week of work, five to-do lists' worth. What will happen? You'll feel rotten. Then you'll start to feel better and get cranky. You'll try to go back to work too fast, but if you're very lucky, someone who loves you will insist that you don't.

Meanwhile, the rest of the world goes right on spinning. Civilization doesn't come to an end. Someone else does your work for you or, more likely, it's not done. Some of the work will still need doing. Miraculously, some of it won't.

You'll have 2,958 messages in your e-mail inbox—2,612 of them spam, and sixty-three of the remaining ones from the same person, the last sixty-two asking why you didn't respond to the first one. Your voice mail will have long since overflowed and stopped taking messages.

You may have a couple of bad days trying to catch up. You'll cope. You always have. If you haven't come back to work too soon, it shouldn't send you into a relapse.

4. *Don't carve the list on stone tablets.*

My first attempts at to-do lists were works of art, carefully proofread and computer printed with crisp black ink on clean ivory paper. I would no more have crossed out or rearranged anything on the list than I would have drawn a mustache on the Mona Lisa.

Your list must be flexible. If that means you write it in pencil, so be it. Maybe you need a dry-erase board, or a stack of index cards for easy shuffling. Choose a format that will encourage you to run the list instead of vice versa.

5. *Order creatively.*

Put the important and urgent tasks at the top of the list. If e-mail is really your top priority, answer it first. If it isn't, and you just want to do it first because it's easy or because you're in the habit, schedule a time to do it later in the day. If a job will nag at you and destroy your concentration until you do it, move it up the list.

Vary long and short jobs, mentally taxing and more routine chores. Change activities and pace often. Attack the mentally challenging jobs when you're most alert and energetic.

6. *Break boulders into pebbles.*

When I first started publishing my newsletter, *Creativity Connection*, I counted backward from the target publication date, allowing time for printing and mailing, and scheduled two large blocks of time on consecutive days to "do newsletter."

Trying to master a computer page design program proved an adventure. Whole pages vanished into the ether, forever to circle the earth with the other space debris. Everything took longer than I anticipated. I worked late trying to wrestle everything onto the pages.

Eventually, I got better at layout, mastered the parts of the computer programs I needed, and learned to write pieces the exact length needed to fill my layout. The newsletter and its editor started to come through the periodic ordeal in much better shape.

I also learned to schedule smaller, more frequent blocks of time to accomplish specific tasks that added up to a finished newsletter. I couldn't lift that boulder of a newsletter all at once, but I could easily tote all the pebbles that comprised it. I've had to master the same pebbles mentality for writing books. Any long-term project requires that kind of planning.

Suppose you've decided that maintaining good physical fitness is one of those "important but not urgent" tasks you've been neglecting. First you need to decide exactly what you mean when you resolve to "exercise regularly."

What sort of exercise? How much? When and where? How often?

Break the boulder-sized goal of exercise into specific activities, based on a realistic appraisal of your capabilities, options, interests, and tolerance for various forms of exercise. You could decide to swim laps for a half hour three times a week, for example, but if you aren't at least an adequate swimmer, like to swim, and have ready access to a pool, you'll never stick with it.

So you settle on these specific tasks:

- ○ Join a health club.
- ○ Walk on a treadmill for thirty minutes three times a week.
- ○ Lift weights three times a week.

You've got a plan. All you need to do is implement it.

"All," he says!

Now's the time to get out the day planner. Schedule around work, home, and your personal obligations and life rhythms. Are you best suited to an early workout on the way to work? Before lunch? Instead of lunch? After work?

When you've decided on times, write them into your calendar and train yourself to consider these "appointments" as important as any others you make. It should require the same sort of emergency that would cause you to miss a doctor's appointment or a board meeting to keep you from your exercise session. Significant injury or illness would of course put the fitness program on temporary hold, but "I don't feel like it" never should.

Be firm in your resolve. Soon the exercise—or any other positive addition to your schedule—will become a happy habit. Give it time to work. It takes at least three weeks to begin to get over the novelty and discomfort of breaking patterns and begin to establish new ones.

Keep referring to your original goals. Are you losing that pound a week you're aiming for? Is your new exercise regimen giving you the increased energy and sense of well-being you hoped for?

Evaluate, too, how the change fits in with the rest of your life. How are your loved ones reacting to this new demand on your time? What have you traded to create time for this new activity? Is it a good swap?

Stick with it for another three weeks. Then make necessary alterations or scrap the plan and develop a new one.

Everything I've just suggested about scheduling exercise goes for any other sort of adjustment you make to your normal routine, including the three in the next step.

7. *Schedule the Three R's: rest, recreation, and relationships.*

You'll rest when everything's finished, right?

But you never really finish everything. There's always something else you could/should be doing—and so you never rest.

Place a rest stop on your daily path where it will do you the most good, before you become tense and exhausted. Brief rests at the right times will help you maintain a steady, efficient work pace. Instead of waiting until the end of the day for a fifteen-minute reading break, for example, schedule it for right after lunch. Or maybe schedule three five-minute breaks instead.

Been promising for weeks to take the kids sledding? Been wanting to take a long walk in the park with your sweetie? Has a "must-read" book been sitting on your bedside table, unopened, for weeks? Put them on your schedule.

Does that sound awful to you? After all, what kind of monster has to schedule playtime with the kids? You're not a monster. You're just too busy. Start planning and scheduling so you can live a balanced, full life.

8. *Schedule long-range as well as short-range goals.*

Can't stand the thought of financial planning for retirement? How about that will you've been meaning to draft?

Many of us shy away from these or other long-range tasks. They're easy to keep postponing, because they fall into that "important but not urgent" category. For these jobs, mañana never seems to come. Schedule time for the non-urgent but vital tasks. You'll feel so good—downright saintly, in fact—when you check them off your list.

9. *Be ready to abandon the list when necessary.*

"If you only write the story that is planned," Ellen Hunnicutt used to tell her creative writing students at the University of

Wisconsin-Madison's School of the Arts at Rhinelander, "you'll miss the story that is revealed."

The same goes for the story of your life. Often the most important events don't appear on the to-do list. Never become so well organized and tightly scheduled that you stop being alert to life's possibilities—the chance encounter, the sudden inspiration.

Not all surprises are bad; not all interruptions are hurtful.

A former colleague used to provide me with a lot of those interruptions. He was a wonderful man, unfailingly kind, gentle, and conscientious. He also functioned in a different time zone than I did. The drummer he marched to kept a much slower beat than mine.

I became quite adept at managing his drop-in visits, deflecting them entirely when time was particularly precious, "managing" him out the door after a few minutes when I was feeling only typically rushed.

But something about the way he stood in the doorway one morning set off a quiet warning in my mind. Instead of giving him the rush treatment, I invited him in and asked him to sit down.

Uncharacteristically, he came right to the point. He had cancer. He had gotten the news a couple of days before, hadn't told anyone except the immediate family. He'd need an operation, and he'd miss work. He wanted me to know, because he considered me to be his friend. Then he admitted he was scared and started to cry.

I expressed my concern and empathy. I reminded him of my wife's happy story. (She's a twenty-year-plus cancer survivor.) I gripped his hands and said a prayer with him.

Mostly, he had just needed to tell someone, to let someone help him carry a crushing weight. He honored me by choosing me for the job. The whole exchange took no more than a few minutes. After he left, I found myself shaking, not only because of his news, but also because of my awareness of how close I had come to turning him away at my door, leaving him alone with his fear.

Nothing on my to-do list that day was nearly as important as spending those few minutes with my friend. I have thanked God many times (but not often enough) for keeping me open to the moment and to a person who needed me. I ask God to help me recognize and seize other opportunities as he gives them to me.

The story has a happy ending. My friend came through the operation fine. He has since retired and moved away, and I miss him. If he ever shows up at my office door again, he'll get a warm welcome, no matter how busy I am.

10. You don't have to make a to-do list at all.

The to-do list, like every other suggestion in this book, is a tool many use in successful time management. If it helps you, use it. If it gets in the way or is more trouble than it's worth, dump it. Don't make a list. Or only make a list on particularly busy, complicated days. You won't be failing time management. You'll be adapting its techniques to suit your temperament, your working style, and your life.

Bonus Suggestion: Create a Not-to-Do List

Along with noting and organizing the tasks you want and need to do, consider making a list of tasks you shouldn't do.

I'm not talking here about pledges to quit smoking or eat less chocolate—as laudable as these goals might be. Not smoking, as those of us who have battled to kick the filthy habit know, isn't at all a matter of doing nothing.

No, this list is for day-to-day tasks you perform out of habit or guilt but that should properly be done by someone else or not done at all. Examine large tasks (serving on the school board) and small ones (responding to every memo from the district manager). Do they need to be done? If so, are you the one who needs to do them? If the answer to either of these questions is no, it's time to get that chore on the not-to-do list and out of your life.

Evaluate how much good you're accomplishing with that noble service on the committee and how much satisfaction you derive from performing it. Balance that with the aggravation and time lost.

You may find lots of material for your not-to-do list. And you may find still more in subsequent chapters on managing machines and regulating the flow of information. But before we get to that, we have one more important item on the agenda, one that I've been meaning to get to but seem to keep putting off. I'm referring, of course, to the fine art of procrastination.

CHAPTER 8

Getting Started

I fully intended to write this chapter weeks ago, but I never got around to it.

It's easy to joke about procrastination. But if you have a tendency to put things off, it's a lot harder to do something about it. If you want to tackle the issue, you first need to understand why you procrastinate in the first place (and the second, third, and fourth places, too, if you're a master procrastinator).

Five Reasons Why You Procrastinate

Reason 1: You haven't really committed to doing the task.

Ever known someone who went into Dad's construction business or sold real estate or became a Marine because someone expected or demanded it? If so, you probably know an unhappy contractor, realtor, or Marine.

We generally don't need to prioritize or otherwise force or trick ourselves into doing things we enjoy. The motivation comes from within, and the reward is in the doing. But if the motivation comes from outside yourself (because someone expects it or asks it or demands it of you), and you don't see a good reason for doing it, you have a much tougher time, and the task becomes work instead of play.

You may chronically put off an activity because you aren't really sold on doing it at all. If that's the case, you need to ask yourself two fundamental questions:

1. What's in it for me if I do it?
2. What will happen to me if I don't?

The answer to the first question can move the motivation from outside to inside. You're no longer doing it because someone said you had to. You're doing it to impress a boss, help a friend, make money, or get to a task you really enjoy, for example.

The second answer is the negative version of the first. Now you're doing the task to avoid something unpleasant, like a lousy job evaluation, an angry or hurt spouse, or a disappointed child. The motivation may be negative, but it still comes from inside you and thus has power.

If you can find no internal motivation—no benefit for doing the job and no penalty for not doing it—you may have discovered a wonderful occasion for practicing those "just say no" skills you developed in chapter 5.

Reason 2: *You're afraid of the job.*

Most of us don't like to admit we're afraid—even to ourselves. But fear may be keeping you from tackling a job that you really want or need to accomplish. If you can identify the source of your reluctance as fear, track it to its source, and face it down, you can then get on with the job.

Here are three of the most common forms of performance anxiety:

1. *Fear of failure*

Consider the student who never studies and subsequently flunks all his classes. He can always tell himself, "If I'd studied,

I would have passed." But what if he studies and still fails? He's lost his excuse.

"Won't" can be a lot easier to accept than "can't." If you don't try something, you'll never have to confront the possibility that you can't do it.

2. Fear of success

What if you not only pass your courses but make straight A's and get on the honor roll? That's great, right? Except that now folks will expect you to do it again. They'll start putting pressure on you to go to college or get that advanced degree or try to get that managerial position.

If you never try, you don't have to face the consequences of success, either.

3. Fear of finishing

If you pass all your courses, you'll graduate. And after you graduate—then what?

For many of the writers I work with, not finishing the novel means you never have to worry about what to do next. You never have to try to get an agent, never have to taste the bitterness of rejection. If you never have a novel published, you'll never have to find out whether anyone would actually buy it. The critics will never have a chance to disparage—or praise—your work.

Not finishing keeps you "safe." You can go right on being all potential. Fear can stop you well short of your goals. Face the fear and act anyway. That's real courage.

Reason 3: *You don't place a high enough priority on the job.*

You agree that somebody ought to do it. If pressed, you might even agree that you're the best person to do it. You may even want to do it. But you just don't want or need to do it enough to make it a priority. You always want or need to do something else more.

You really do need to clean out the garage. You'd be embarrassed to have anyone else do it for you and see the mess you've made! But still the garage remains a toxic waste dump week after week. This sort of procrastination may work itself out. As other tasks get done, the low priority job may become high priority—especially if you buy a new car and really want to have a garage to put it in.

Take a look at the job you're avoiding and see if you can recast it in terms of the ultimate benefit you'll get for doing it. For example, "If I don't clean out the garage, I won't have anyplace to put the new car (or even the old beater) to get it out of the weather."

That's negative. Positive motivation tends to be stronger. Recast the statement in positive form:

"If I clean out the garage, I'll have a place for the car—finally!"

Then consider the side benefits:

○ You'll stop worrying about it.
○ Your dear husband/wife will stop worrying you about it.
○ You'll get some exercise.
○ You can listen to the ball game or music while you work.

This reasoning recently got me through a long-overdue clean-up of my own garage, by the way. I do try to take my own advice.

Reason 4: *You don't know enough to do the job right.*

What writers mistakenly label as "writer's block" is often simply the subconscious mind's way of telling us we don't know enough to write what should come next. This is true of other motivational blocks, too. You may not yet know enough to do the job right. You haven't consciously recognized or admitted this, but you know it on a deeper level, and this awareness pops up as a strong aversion that fuels procrastination. Seek out the information you need. If all else fails, read the directions (a desperate last resort for many men, myself included).

A cautionary note: seek only as much information as you need. Eternal research can be another way of putting off a task, and reading about how to do something is a lot easier than doing it. You could always know more. Learn what you need, and then get to work.

Reason 5: *You just plain don't want to!*

On a preference scale of one to ten, one being "I'd rather die" and ten being "let me at it," trying to remove burrs from my dog Sprecher rates about a minus two. It's unpleasant. It's messy. It's even dangerous. (He *really* doesn't like to get burrs picked off!) It's torture for both of us, and nobody comes out of it happy.

When you confront a minus-two job, you've got three choices, and you don't need a book on time management to tell you what they are:

1. You can leave the job undone,
2. You can pay someone else to do it, or
3. You can hitch up your pants and do it yourself.

Decide and act or choose not to act and accept the consequences. If the third option is the best, despite your misgivings, then go ahead and do it.

Seven Ways to Get a Fast Start

The problem of procrastination doesn't always end when you identify its source, confront it, and steel yourself for the task at hand. That still leaves the stalling we get so good at when facing an odious task.

Here are three tips for preparing yourself in advance of the job, three more for actually beginning, and one for sustaining the momentum if you can't finish it.

Preparing for the Job

1. Prepare mentally.

In 1912, Charles Haanel wrote *The Master Key System* of successful living. His guarantee was simple, straightforward, and all-inclusive: "The Master Key will help you solve your problems." He called the subconscious mind "a benevolent stranger, working on your behalf." After all the subsequent research on creativity and brain theory, I've never read a better description of the mystery we call "inspiration."

Haanel asserted that we can recruit that benevolent stranger to work for us whenever we need it. You simply tell your subconscious exactly what you want to accomplish. You don't issue orders. You don't tell the subconscious how to do the job. You simply plant the idea and give that larger mind outside of conscious thought time to mull and sift and play. Your "benevolent stranger" will combine images and ideas, amass energy, and generate enthusiasm for the project.

"Positive visualization," right? Whatever you call it, it really does work. Erase the negative mental disaster tapes that contribute so heavily to the fear and loathing that may accompany some challenges for you. Instead, show success stories in the theater of your mind.

2. Prepare physically.

Before beginning, make sure you have at hand all the tools you need. When you schedule the time, also stake out the place. When you designate a particular place for the work, your mind will learn to become focused and ready every time you return to that space.

If the challenge will require more than one session, try to find a space where you can leave everything you need right where you put it down. You will eliminate time spent pitching camp and tearing it down again every time you work on the project.

3. Map your terrain.

Before you begin the trip, remind yourself where you want to go and review how you intend to get there. Why are you accepting this challenge? What do you hope to accomplish? Focus on the goal.

If the work involves several steps, write them down first. I'm not talking about a formal outline with Roman numerals, just a simple list. If you aren't sure of the proper sequence, note them in the order they occur to you. Then number them as you go along.

If you're preparing for a task you've done many times before (but still tend to put off), these three preliminary steps need take only a few seconds, and they're well worth doing. Take a breath. You're ready to begin. The next three steps will help you get off to a flying start.

Beginning the Job

4. Start anywhere.

Some jobs don't need to be performed in proper sequence. If you're not ready to begin at the beginning, begin somewhere else.

When a director makes a movie, for example, she'll shoot scenes out of proper sequence. She'll schedule all the scenes from a particular location at the same time, for example. The same goes for all the scenes in which the hero appears with a full beard and the ones in which a superstar makes a cameo appearance. Then the editor puts everything in proper order to tell a coherent story.

Some tasks, of course, must be performed in proper order. A plumber has to turn off the water before removing pipes. But other jobs are flexible enough to allow you a choice of starting points.

It may not matter *where* you start; it only matters *that* you start—which brings us to:

5. *Start anyway.*

Some writers fall prey to what they call a "block." Poets seem especially susceptible to this malady. Deadline writers never get a block. They write when they feel rotten. They write when they don't want to. They write when they're preoccupied. No matter what, they write. Perhaps they use positive visualization. Perhaps they visualize themselves in the unemployment line if they don't start tapping the keys. Whatever they do, they write. The same goes for "plumber's block," "airline pilot's block," and most especially "parent's block."

Do the job, whether you feel inspired or not. If you know what you're doing and give it your best effort, neither your mood nor your motivation (or lack thereof) will show in the finished product. Nobody will be able to tell if you felt like doing it or not. Fact is, people don't care. They're interested in the results, and those results can be good regardless of your mental state when you created them.

6. *Lock out the critics.*

We all make mistakes. Most of us get to make ours in private, and we often have a chance to fix them before anyone even knows. Others aren't so fortunate. When Brett Favre threw an interception for the Green Bay Packers (and he threw plenty of them, as great as he was), half the known universe saw him do it (or so it seemed if you live in Wisconsin). He couldn't take the pass back and throw it over.

I know writers who compose rough drafts as if a whole stadium full of rabid fans and millions more TV viewers were watching their every key peck. Even worse, they seem to hear their editors, English teachers, and other vocal critics shouting at them from the sidelines, just waiting to pounce on every fumbled verb.

But writing—like most other jobs—is a two-step process. First you do it, and then you (and others) evaluate it. After judging, you may refine and modify it. In the initial stage of creative work, you need to shut out all concerns about future judgments. If you don't, you'll see failure in the eyes of that invisible arbiter, and that fear will prevent you from doing your best work—assuming you can even start at all.

Keep the Momentum Going

If you have to leave off before you can finish the project, here's a final step to help you begin quickly the next time you resume.

7. Stop before you need to.

Momentum gives you a wonderful feeling, especially when you've got a lot to do and little time to do it. When you're on a roll, the last thing you want is an interruption. Common sense tells you to ride that wave as far as it will carry you.

If you keep working too long, you may become exhausted or run into a barrier that stymies you. You quit with the job in pieces, and you carry that mess around in your mind, where it turns into dread at having to come back and pick up those pieces later.

If you tend to be great at starting but not so great at finishing, and you leave lots of projects half done, this could be the problem. It makes a lot more sense to stop before you're exhausted or stuck. Stop in midstride (literally in midsentence for a writer), sure of the next step you'll take. You'll return to the job confident, maybe even eager. You don't have to waste time getting back into the groove because you won't have gotten out of it.

You now have a simple seven-step plan to help you plunge into any task that needs doing. But what about all the other tasks you shouldn't be doing at all? Eliminating them lies at the core of effective time management. In the next two chapters, I'll show you how to manage all the machines that complicate your life and to stem the flow of information that threatens to drown you.

Ready? No procrastination. Let's do it!

CHAPTER 9

Managing the Machines

When Alexander Graham Bell invented the telephone, he immediately rang up his assistant in the next room and summoned him. We've been dancing to the telephone's tune ever since. Cell phones are everywhere, including, alas, theaters, restaurants, and churches. The ringing of the cell phone has become as irritating to diners as secondhand smoke.

Commercial airlines and rental cars come equipped with phones. You can buy them from vending machines in California. Can cellular phone implants be far off? (Oh, I hope so!)

We can speed dial and automatically redial. We have call forwarding, call waiting, and call blocking. Voice mail will preserve any incoming call we somehow manage to miss—whether we want it or not.

We have all this, it often seems, primarily so we can tell one another where we are now and how soon we'll get to someplace else.

Sometimes when we try to reach someone by phone, we instead get a digitized voice telling us:

If you wish to schedule a service appointment, press 1.

If your request is an emergency, press 2.

If you need to speak to a service representative, good luck.

The telephone is a prime example of technology run amok, through abuse and overuse. It's an incredibly helpful tool, as are the computer, the Internet, GPS, and all the other modern marvels we so quickly learn to take for granted. But we need to make sure that we're the masters of technology and not its slaves. To do so, we need to calculate the real time and energy costs of all our gadgets.

Tallying the True Tariff of Technology

1. The time it takes to select it

The tale of the telephone. Once upon a time, children, back when the world was young, the telephone was black and had a dial. (Funny that we still refer to "dialing" the telephone. Young folks have never even seen a rotary phone.) Your only choice when you bought a phone was whether you wanted the extra-long cord to attach it to the wall. (Yes, children, phones needed to be plugged in then, and you couldn't even take the receiver off its pod and walk around with it.)

There wasn't a lot of flexibility, true, but it sure made getting a phone easier.

Now we have choices. Oh, boy, do we have choices—not only of shape, size, and capabilities of the phone, but of which company and which service plan to opt for. Choice is good. We all like choice. But choice takes time and energy and can be confusing, even bewildering.

2. The time it takes to learn how to use it

That old-fashioned telephone didn't come with a user's manual. Nobody needed to be told how to use the phone. You picked up the receiver, got the dial tone, and dialed the number or spoke to the operator who connected you.

Now, of course, everything comes with instructions, often neither brief nor concise, sometimes incomprehensible. Brewing a cup of coffee has become a learning experience—

when perhaps all you really wanted was a cup of coffee.

When you calculate whether a piece of technology helps you, remember to count the time you spend crawling up the slippery slope of the learning curve, along with the time lost making mistakes.

3. The time it takes to get it fixed and upgraded

You do in time learn to master the machine (some of us much faster than others). You and the toy become an efficient team. Then one horrible morning, you push the button or flip the switch, and nothing happens—or, worse, lots of things start happening, all of them bad.

Your partner, your pal, has gone on strike.

Some of us get quite good at using the machines, but very few of us can even attempt to repair them. The only "cure" I've ever perfected is a simple three-step procedure I always follow when my computer has a seizure. First I yell at it. Then I thump it with my open hand. If that fails, I reboot (turn it off and then on again).

If these techniques, as subtle and refined as they are, fail to restore life, I have to get help, wait for help to arrive, and pay for that help. We call the intervals spent waiting "downtime" for good reason. We cannot function without our fabulous toys.

4. Dealing with downtime

As we master the technology, we also come to rely on it. Years ago, I wrote books on an electric typewriter. (You remember the typewriter, that marvelous machine of legend that produced "hard copy" right out of its top.) I'm even old enough to have pecked pages and pages on a manual type-writer. ("Look, Ma! No plug!") I had a tough time adapting to an electric typewriter, let alone to a computer.

While I may get nostalgic thinking about my grandfather's old manual typewriter, I would never, ever want to go back to using one! Now that I've learned to operate the computer, I love it! It makes me a better writer, because I revise more now. I'm more willing to take chances with my writing because the penalty for being wrong is a simple touch of the delete key.

Even if I wanted to go back to the typewriter, as far as I know the last store in Madison that sold and serviced them went out of business years ago.

Oh, but when the computer chokes on a byte or the power goes out, *I'm* out of business!

So, along with the purchase price, the true cost of technology must include:

○ buying time;
○ learning time;
○ maintenance time;
○ downtime.

But don't we get that lost time back in increased efficiency? After all, along with the "paperless office," the computer was supposed to usher in the Age of Leisure, when our biggest problem would be spending all the free time the machines save us.

What happened to all that time? Like the money I saved when I stopped smoking, it seemed to evaporate. Here are three reasons why.

Where the "Saved Time" Really Went

1. The fallacy of increased expectations

Instead of decreasing the amount of time we spend creating the report, we've increased the size and complexity of a report and the number of reports we're supposed to create. We've swapped "saved time" for "increased productivity," all in the name of achieving a higher standard of living for ourselves and our families.

2. The last-minute syndrome

When we had to rely on surface mail, we knew to set our deadlines accordingly. Overnight mail allowed us to push the deadline back a day or two. The fax machine let us wait until the next-to-last minute, and e-mail lets us transmit material as we write it (often a big mistake!). None of this saves us any time; it simply allows us to put tasks off longer.

3. The if-you-build-it-they-will-come phenomenon

When we build a bypass to ease traffic jams on a road, cars flock to the bypass. Traffic soon clogs the new road, and we begin drawing up plans for a bypass to the bypass.

In the same way, the volume of communication expands to fill the channels we create for it. All this adds up to a big problem: the technology that was supposed to free us has bound us ever tighter in the time trap. Here's how to get out of that trap:

Three Tips for Taming Technology

1. Buy only what you need.

The arms race—that global insanity that had the former Soviet Union and the United States stockpiling nuclear armaments until we could destroy each other and the rest of the world several times over—may have eased, but many of us still engage in the gigabyte race.

Your beautiful new computer suddenly becomes obsolete the moment someone unveils the newer, flashier, more powerful model. But has your machine really become deficient just because a more advanced one hit the market? If the technology still does what you want and need it to do, you don't need a newer, "better" one.

2. *Learn only what you need to know.*

I can drive a car with a stick shift or an automatic transmission. I know how to fill it with gasoline and clean the windshield. And I know Dean's phone number. He's my car service rep. I could no more fix the engine than I could flap my arms and fly. I let Dean and his crew do it.

I don't understand how computers work, either. I can write and edit my manuscripts and create page layouts for my newsletter. Granted, I don't know how to do all the tricks my design program can do, but I know how to do everything I want and need to do. When I need to do more, I'll learn more—but not until then.

3. *Create communication-free zones.*

Do you really need to be on-call 24/7? Do you have to answer every ringing telephone, respond to every e-mail the moment it arrives? Some people, like a doctor on call, really do have to be that accessible. But for me, that kind of accessibility would be an indulgence, a way to feel important, perhaps even a means of putting off real work. I generally respond to my students and answer their questions within a day (Sundays excepted), and when I know I'll be otherwise occupied, I warn them of any possible delay. My online novel-writing students seldom have plot synopsis emergencies, at least nothing that can't wait an hour or two, so that's almost always good enough.

I establish e-mail and telephone-free times in my workday because I need to do other work (like thinking). And when I'm ready to lay my burden down for the day, I need to be able to get away from my work.

Just as you must manage the machines in your life, you also need to stem the flow of information the machines now bring you, which threatens to engulf us all. In the next chapter, we'll share tips on how to avoid being washed away in a flood of facts—true or false.

CHAPTER 10

Managing Information

We now have all of the world's knowledge literally at our fingertips. With a laptop computer and wireless connection to the Internet, we can go anywhere and still have access to all the marvelous search engines. We don't have to know anything, because we can ask anything online. That's the good news.

The bad news is, we also have access to tons of stuff we'd never want or need in a hundred lifetimes, and we often have to wade through oceans of it to get to what we do want. And when we get there, a lot of what we find is inaccurate, and some of it is flat-out nonsense.

When seeking information, we must find the good stuff while avoiding the bad, the irrelevant, the inane, and, most important, the convincing but wrong. As someone once said, "It ain't what we don't know that gets us into trouble. It's what we know for sure that ain't so."

You don't even have to go looking for misinformation. If you use e-mail, it will find you. For example:

> WARNING: ALIENS HAVE BEEN ABDUCTING UN-WARY TRAVELERS, PUTTING THEM INTO A TRANCE, AND REMOVING A KIDNEY TO SELL ON THE BLACK MARKET. THIS IS NOT A JOKE! IT'S REAL!
> FORWARD THIS MESSAGE TO TEN FRIENDS IMMEDI-ATELY OR YOUR KIDNEY COULD BE NEXT!

These alerts generally come from well-meaning friends and are often prefaced with the words "I usually don't forward things like this, but..."

Hit delete and wait for the apologetic follow-up: "Sorry. It turns out it was just a scam. I sure thought..."

Along with the scam, we have spam, that endless barrage of solicitations for low-interest loans, weight-reduction schemes, and "business opportunities." A lot of folks are trying to steal our identities. For example, a message that claims to come from your bank tells you there's a problem with your account, and you need to provide your security information immediately so they can rectify it.

Responding to such pernicious garbage could lose you your good name along with your money. Spam costs virtually nothing to send, and the scammer only has to fool one person in a million to make it pay. Sure, you're smart enough to recognize spam when you see it, but the sheer volume of the stuff takes time to sift through and delete. And once you separate the garbage from the stuff you really want, you still need to verify whether it's good information or eyewash. Here's how:

Five Ways to Verify the Validity of Information

1. Consider the source.

Always ask, "Says who?" Notoriety is not the same as credibility; even well-known and widely quoted sources can be wrong.

2. Track down the ultimate source.

By the time you get it, information may have passed through many computers, filtered by many minds. See if you can trace it back to its origin.

3. Check the date.

Like milk and yogurt, information has a shelf life and can spoil. Just as you check the "best if purchased before" date on a carton of cottage cheese, check to see when the site was last updated.

4. Separate fact from opinion.

If I tell you it's raining, you can verify the accuracy of my statement. Thus, it's a factual statement—even if it's wrong and the sun is shining. You can check, verify, even ultimately prove or disprove such a statement.

If I tell you the weather stinks, we could argue forever without proving anything. Ducks allegedly love rain, and so do some people. "Stinks" is an opinion, and you can never ascertain the truth of an opinion, only the facts it's based on.

5. Cross-check your sources.

When I went to journalism school, a professor taught me, "If your mother says she loves you, get a second source." A tad cynical, perhaps, but you get the point. Like a good reporter, check information against a second and even a third source. If you find disagreement, keep checking until you have a reliable consensus.

Will keeping a bar of soap under the covers really prevent leg cramps at night? Was Mr. Rogers really a decorated war hero? Go to Snopes.com or other Web sites that deal with debunking urban myths to test the validity of such claims.

Three Ways to Avoid Drowning in Information

If it's all there and so easy to access, then we should know more and more, right? The Internet has spawned its own psychological syndrome, information anxiety, the ever-increasing gap between what we know and what we think we ought to know.

Even before you verify the information, make sure you really need it in the first place. To stem the tide of information, follow these three tips:

1. Give yourself permission not to know everything about everything.

What's the weather like in Zanzibar, Tanzania? I could find out in seconds. Do I really need to know, or am I just putting off the work I should be doing?

Checking the world's weather is easy and fun. It requires discipline to turn from fun to hard work. If you later discover that you really do need to know climate conditions in Zanzibar, you can always check then.

2. Rip, read, and recycle.

Train yourself to skim for main ideas and scan for specific information. Take only what you need. With the time you save skimming and scanning, you'll be able to savor a bedtime story with your kid or read aloud a favorite poem just for you.

Don't print it unless you're sure you'll need it later. Once you generate a piece of paper, you have to tend it, and tending takes time.

3. Create a "to-read" file for waiting rooms.

You don't have to visit the doctor to get stuck in a waiting room. They're everywhere, even in your own home. When someone keeps you waiting, pull out your "to-read" file and fill that wait with meaning, enjoyment, or both.

When you stem the flood of information, you're still left with a truth that predates the Internet by centuries: information isn't the same as knowledge, and knowledge doesn't equal wisdom. It's quite possible that we understand less and less as we know more and more.

That said, the Internet is a marvelous tool; as a writer, teacher, and curious human being, I wouldn't be without it. We shouldn't spurn it and go back to relying solely on Mr. Dewey and his mighty decimals just because the Internet provides us ready access to so many "You just might be a redneck if…" jokes, cartoons, and porn sites. It can just as easily grant us access to Bible studies, Lenten reflections, and the wisdom of Thomas Merton. And, if used properly, it can even save us time.

In the next chapter, we'll take a little of that saved time and turn it into a mini-vacation, or four of them, actually, every day. Then, in the following chapter, we'll focus on time you spend waiting—waiting in line, waiting in traffic jams, and waiting for the phone to ring. You can use these "spare" shards of time to relax and refresh yourself.

CHAPTER 11

The Power of the Pause

When I was a kid, summer revolved around Dad's two-week vacation. We usually spent it near a mountain lake, where Dad would fish while God's nature refreshed his weary mind and body and renewed his soul.

How he must have looked forward to those two weeks out of fifty-two. I'm sure he also looked forward to the weekends he spent with my brother and me, camping, fishing, hiking, and going to ball games.

We all need vacations, but if you wait fifty weeks to take one, it will be too late to free you from stress, exhaustion, and inefficiency. Even pausing for the weekend isn't enough. You really need to take at least four vacations every day. We're talking about extremely short vacations; a ninety-second break can be incredibly rejuvenating.

Don't wait to be exhausted, frustrated, or stuck. You should take breaks even before you feel you need them. Break the momentum and the buildup of stress and fatigue with a regular sanity break.

Here are seven ways to take a mini-vacation without straying from home, school, or office, the cab of your truck, or wherever you happen to be:

The Seven Sanctifying Sanity Breaks

1. The breath break

When you feel hurried and pressured, your breathing becomes shallow. You might become mildly oxygen deprived. The yawn you thought signified boredom may actually be your body struggling to get more air.

The breath break is the easiest and cheapest vacation you'll ever take. Mentally step away from your work for two minutes and just breathe. Take the air deep into your belly. You don't have to take a workshop on how to breathe. You don't have to chant a mantra or count your breaths. You don't even have to make noise. (You can take a stealthy breath break right in the middle of a meeting or class.)

Just breathe.

2. The prison break

Think of a place where you once felt peace and contentment. "Most people long for another island," Bloody Mary sings in *South Pacific*. "One where they know they will like to be." Or make one up. What does heaven look like for you? Imagine it in rich detail.

Like my father, I've found my greatest peace beside mountain lakes: Clear Lake, in the Gallatin Range of the Rocky Mountains of Montana; Crystal Lake, in the San Gabriel Mountains of Southern California; Columbine Lake, near Estes Park, Colorado. I consider them sacred places.

Go rest in one of your sacred places for a couple of minutes. Shut everything else out. Close your eyes if circumstances allow. Create the scene. See, hear, smell, and feel it. Let peace flow over and through you.

You'll return refreshed.

3. The exorcism

What—or who—is bothering you?

Something's lurking just below consciousness, making you distracted and irritable. Instead of trying to lock it out and ignore it, invite it into conscious thought. Picture it clearly. If it's an abstract, like "lack of time," create a concrete image, like a clock gone berserk, its hands spinning out of control.

Live with the image for a minute or two and then banish it. Create a bubble around it and let it float away; watch it get smaller and smaller in your mental sky until it disappears. If that's too gentle, blow it into tiny bits! You might even enjoy this. Hey, isn't that what vacations are for?

4. The shrug

We tend to take our tensions out on specific parts of our bodies. By the end of a hard day, we develop gut aches, back spasms, eye twitches, or perhaps a stabbing pain in the jaw. I tend to abuse my shoulders. Without even knowing it, I tense up as I work. If I don't stop in time, I get a sore neck and shoulders, which in turn produce a pounding headache.

I break the tension, save my shoulders, avert the headache, and deflate my stress by relaxing my shoulders (I can feel them drop) and slowly, gently rotating them for a couple of minutes. It's incredibly refreshing. On a rough day, I might need to do this again in a couple of hours. Each time I do, I relieve the pain and break the stress cycle.

Find your trouble spot and send it some love for a couple of minutes. At the end of the day, you'll notice the difference.

5. The mini-meditation

Read or recall a line of Scripture, a favorite poem, or something someone said to you that struck you as particularly wise and worthy of reflection. Repeat it and reflect on it for a minute or two, letting your mind follow its own course.

I jot down such good prompts in a little notebook I carry with me, so I'll always have something to focus on. Keeping a Bible handy is of course always a good idea, and it's an inexhaustible source of food for thought.

6. *The object of your affection reflection*

Imagine the face of a loved one. Hold the person up to God, thanking him for that person's presence in your life. Call up a favorite memory of that person.

7. *Graduate level mini-vacation*

Try combining the breath break with any of the other vacations. Breathe deeply and slowly while you mentally journey to one of your sacred places, for example.

The 21-Day Guarantee

At first you'll probably need to remind yourself to take these "vacations." (Here again, sticky notes or preprogrammed computer prompts can be helpful.) You may feel self-conscious or even foolish about taking them. Don't quit after a couple of tries, don't abandon the plan if you miss a couple of breaks, and don't make the process complicated and onerous, one more to-do on the list. Keep it simple and enjoyable and just keep doing it, whether it seems to be working or not.

Remember, it takes at least three weeks to establish a new habit pattern. Try this vacation plan for twenty-one days before you judge how it's affecting you. If after twenty-one days you decide it's not working for you, you've given it a fair test and should try something else. I'm betting that won't be the case, though. If you try them, I think you'll like these mini-vacations very much and will make them a positive habit, a wonderful part of each day.

For when "vacations" are forced on you each day by people who keep you waiting, the next section will offer some tips for turning frustration into refreshment and accomplishment.

Turning the Wait into a Rest

How long has it been since you've been bored?

I can recall the endless summer afternoons of childhood: I'm tired of reading and riding my bike around the neighborhood. Nothing's on the radio but Mom's soap operas. My best friend, Craig Marvel, had to take his little brother, Eric, to the barber, and nobody's around to play with. It's still hours before Dad will come home and play catch with me in the yard.

"Mom! I'm bored! There's nothing to do!"

There was plenty to do, of course, including chores around the house and yard, but nothing I wanted to do. I probably needed a nap—but was of course much too old (and too young) for such nonsense.

I remember, too, how restless I was in the days leading up to Christmas. Remember trying to get through an endless Christmas Eve afternoon?

As adults, we always have something (or five or six somethings) needing to be done and not enough time to do them, plus all those things we wish we could do "if only we had the time." We have no time for boredom—but we still get restless, irritable, distracted, and impatient, especially when someone or something keeps us waiting.

Waiting is an inevitable fact of modern life. We're all in a hurry, and we're all trying to get someplace else. We invariably get in one another's way. No matter what line at the market or lane on the highway you choose, it always seems to be the slow-est. You seem to always be behind the person at the post office who wants to send a package overseas and pay the postage in pennies.

You can try to avoid making appointments with the folks in your life who are chronically late. You can plan your errands to avoid peak traffic times. Most importantly, you can create a realistic to-do list, allowing for the waits, so they won't destroy your carefully crafted schedule.

But no matter how carefully you plan, others will make you wait—just as you'll make them wait for you. Accept the inevitability of the wait and learn to turn it into positive, productive time.

Renaming the Wait

What if you called it a rest instead of a wait?

The driver ahead of you in traffic slows down while the left turn arrow is still green, creeps through the intersection on the yellow, and oozes obliviously away while you sulk and fester at the red light.

You can call the guy a moron (or worse) and pound the steering wheel. That won't get the signal to change to green any faster, and you might spike your blood pressure. It certain-ly won't teach that other driver the lesson you're so sure he or she richly deserves. But you can react that way if you choose to.

Or you can choose to thank the driver for the opportunity to take a mini-vacation. You'll still have to wait, but by turning the wait into a rest, you can make it a positive experience. That's up to you.

You can also transform longer waits into productive times. If the meeting never starts on time, bring your mail and go through it while you wait. Take out a notepad or laptop and do some brainstorming. Plan a week's worth of menus. Write a haiku. Conduct a mental dialogue with someone you've always wanted to talk to. Pray. Meditate on Scripture. If you're stuck in the doctor's waiting room and forgot to bring a paperback or crossword puzzle, read one of those moldy magazines. Try something you'd never ordinarily read, perhaps a craft magazine or a children's publication, and get a new perspective on life.

You'll be less stressed and better read. You'll return to the wars more efficient and effective. And you might write a great haiku or solve a problem that's been nagging you for weeks. You may as well do something you want or need to do. You're going to wait the same amount of time either way, but this way, it'll seem a lot shorter.

I hope you're able to avoid some of the waits and put the rest to good use. In the next chapter, we'll explore ways to keep you from wasting anyone else's time.

CHAPTER 12

Managing
Other People's Time

In the prayer that Jesus taught us, we're directed to ask for the Father's forgiveness *as we forgive others*. We will be judged, Jesus tells us, by the same measure we use to judge others.

Remember also the wise rabbi who summed up all the law and the prophets with what we call the Golden Rule: "Do to others as you would have them do to you."

Just as we don't want others to waste our time—by keeping us waiting, putting needless items on our daily agenda, or otherwise inconveniencing us—we should be wary of wasting other folks' time as well.

We don't like people to ask questions like, "Got a minute?" If someone asks for a few moments of your precious time, you'd like to know exactly how many moments they want and what they want them for. In the same way, we should give others the information they need to make an informed response to our questions.

Not: "Are you busy?"

But: "Is there some time today when you'd be available for ten minutes to review our strategy for tomorrow's meeting?"

Here are seven more tips for doing unto others what you would have them do unto you:

1. *Never waste their time.*

This is, of course, the prime directive; all the others flow from it. If the sight of one of your workers standing idle threatens you, resist the temptation to assign busywork. The worker will know the "job" for what it is, and trust in and respect for you will erode.

In the same way, if your kids seem to be sitting around doing nothing, it isn't your job to entertain or divert them. Creativity can arise from boredom! Give them a chance to invent their own activity.

Don't fill time for others. Show them what needs doing. If necessary, show them how to do it. Then get out of their way.

2. *Make sure they have the tools they need to do the job.*

And make sure those tools are in proper working order. Often, as boss, your job is to serve and facilitate. Make sure, too, that they don't have more tools than they need. As we've seen, technology can be a wonderful servant but a terrible master—for those who work with you as well as for you. Do they really need to learn a new system?

For that matter, will new office policies and procedures facilitate work or get in the way? What about that bulky document outlining "How to write a mission statement?" Or all those FYI e-mail attachments?

Provide such "gifts" sparingly, with common sense. Your workers will appreciate the ones they get much more—and appreciate you for not wasting their time.

3. *Separate the important from the merely urgent for others.*

The e-mail program I use at work enables the sender to attach an exclamation point to the subject line of a message to indicate that it's "top priority." One of my colleagues tends to flag every message with a "!"—including the reminder of the coffee break in room 726 tomorrow at 10:00 A.M.—everyone invited! Needless to say, I no longer get excited when I see the "!" on e-mail from that person.

Before you grab the phone or issue a memo demanding immediate attention and response, ask yourself if it's really necessary. If so, does it really need a response right away? Relieve pressure and release coworkers to tackle the top-priority items on their to-do lists.

If you don't, the next time you cry "Urgent!" no one will believe you.

4. *Allow them enough time for the task.*

Just as you need to be realistic when you plan your own day, be reasonable in your demands on others. If you make it impossible for them to do a good job or to even finish the job in the time you allot for it, you'll encourage shoddy work and get folks into the habit of falling short. You'll also find yourself spending a lot of your own time policing, poking, and prodding others instead of tending to your own work. Everybody loses.

5. *Tell them why.*

My father told a story about the two men digging ditches side by side at a construction site.

A curious passer-by asks the first, "What are you doing?"

The sweaty worker looks up, glares, and snarls, "I'm digging a ditch! What does it look like I'm doing?"

Undaunted, the passer-by asks the second man the same question.

Equally sweaty, he looks up, smiles, and says, "I'm helping to build a cathedral."

Same job. Very different attitude. The second worker knows the goal and thus the importance of the menial job he is performing.

People generally do much better work when they understand its purpose. When you ask someone to do something, also provide a good reason. You'll have a more willing and efficient helper. If you can't come up with a good reason, maybe you shouldn't be asking at all.

If the question, "Why do I have to do this?" sounds like a threat to your authority and puts you on the defensive, your attitude needs some adjusting. People might stop asking, but they won't stop wondering.

6. Encourage "monotasking."

Our kids can teach us a lot about concentration. The child who seems to have the attention span of a hyperactive flea when reading a textbook can lose herself in Harry Potter books or *The Chronicles of Narnia* for hours without coming up for air. Practice the scales? Drudgery. "Practice" video games? Bring it on! He'll "work" with single-minded devotion, screening out all distractions (such as you telling him to wash up for dinner).

Encourage and reward the sort of concentration on task that comes so naturally to children doing something they enjoy. You shouldn't be teaching a child or colleague to multitask any more than you should be demanding it of yourself.

That applies to the "power" or working lunch. Even if you can only provide a short lunch break, give workers a real break from work.

7. Cut down on meetings.

Ask the staff to list the urgent but not important tasks in their daily grind, and chances are meetings will be high on most everybody's list. The same might be true of family meetings. And for many people I know, hearing a spouse say, "Honey, we need to talk" makes the blood run cold.

Don't call a meeting unless you have a good reason to meet. If you have a meeting scheduled but find yourself struggling to come up with agenda items, cancel the meeting. (Have you ever heard anyone complain because a meeting was scrapped?)

That said, sometimes there's no effective substitute for getting people together. When everyone is in the same room (or on the same conference call, at least), everyone hears the same thing at the same time, eliminating some (but, alas, not all) miscommunication. If folks don't understand something, they can say so—and keep talking until they do. Most importantly, when they interact, people generate ideas that they might never have come up with separately. The whole is often greater than the sum of its parts.

Plan that meeting carefully, have everything you need before you start, and keep the pace brisk. People will still complain about meetings, of course. It's part of our culture, and we think it's expected of us. But they won't really hate them—and might even enjoy them.

Now that we've spent some time making sure you don't waste other peoples' time, let's get back to managing yours by beginning to cut through the mess that might be gumming up the works.

CHAPTER 13

Clutter Control

How much time do you waste looking for stuff?

Oh, but you know exactly where everything is, right? That's what I used to tell people, too, when they would step in at my office door, gasp, and quickly step back into the hall, muttering, "Oh, my!" or "Excuse me, I must have the wrong office. This is obviously the unsanitary landfill."

Along with predictions that the computer would usher in the age of leisure, we were supposed to achieve the paperless office long ago. But if anything, computers have created more paper, which means we spend more time processing it. ("Process" sometimes means transferring it from the interoffice mail envelope to the recycling basket, but even that takes time.)

I'm still a prime offender in the clutter category. (I figure every horizontal surface, including the floor, is a potential filing cabinet.) But I'm trying, and I'm getting better about building levees to control my flood of paper. Here are a few tips that have helped me.

Seven Ways to Control Catastrophic Clutter

1. Adopt a constant companion.

Keep a notebook with you at all times. When you get a sudden inspiration or see something in the newspaper you're keen on remembering, use your notebook instead of scribbling on a scrap of paper, tearing the story out of the newspaper or, worse yet, keeping the whole newspaper section.

When you get a meeting reminder or announcement for something you want to attend, note it on your calendar right away, with pertinent contact information. If you still need to hang onto the announcement, do so, of course, but if you can pitch it, so much the better.

2. *Create a pile for everything and everything in its pile.*

I'm never going to have what anyone might call a pristine desktop, either the literal one or my computer screen, but I'm learning to use folders, real and virtual, with clear, simple labels. It's helping a lot—as long as I don't let too many folders and piles build up.

3. *Exercise good sortsmanship.*

I've tried to follow the "only touch each piece of paper once" admonition popular in so many time management texts. I've failed. If you can do it, more power to you. But I do try to make a decision about a piece of paper or material on a Web site the first time I encounter it. Toss it? (You can usually toss envelopes immediately, even if you need to keep the contents.) Read and deal with it right now? Label and file it? Reroute it to someone else? (It belongs to whoever touched it last, right?) Put it in the "to read" folder for the next time you find yourself waiting?

Make your decision and move on.

4. *Strip, clip, and flip.*

Cut out the material you want from a publication and recycle the rest right away. Also recycle periodicals and memos you haven't looked at in a year (unless there's some legal reason why you should keep them longer, as with tax records).

5. Question the need.

The next time you get a renewal reminder for a periodical, ask yourself if you still read, want, or need the publication. Eliminate bookmarks you no longer use on the Internet. Unsubscribe to online newsletters you never seem to get around to reading.

Before you file that next piece of paper, ask yourself if you're ever really likely to need or read it again.

6. Shift gears when you read.

Many of us read everything at one consistent speed (slow). From the Sunday funnies to the annual report, we plod along, word by word, whether we need only the main idea, the basic facts, or every detail. But you can train yourself to skim, scan, and read quickly, depending on your need.

That doesn't negate the times when you want to read carefully or even read aloud for rhythm and sound. But let's face it—how many annual reports have rhythm?

7. Purge.

Even your best efforts at following the previous six guidelines might still leave you with a compost heap of paper. If so, set a time at the end of every workday, the end of the week, once a month—frequency depends on how fast your compost accumulates—to plow through the pile, tossing, sorting, and rerouting. An added bonus: you'll find items you need to respond to but would otherwise have forgotten.

Try as many of these tips as seem helpful to you. Cut yourself a large slice of slack whenever you slip back into old slovenly ways. If you stick with it, in time you'll develop some helpful habits.

CHAPTER 14

Honoring Thy Body Rhythms

All God's children got rhythm.

Even if you can't dance, you've been endowed by your Creator with your own body rhythm, called the circadian rhythm, which regulates your peak times of high energy. Most of us experience two peaks and two corresponding troughs during each twenty-four-hour cycle. My peaks aren't necessarily the same as yours (which is why there are "morning people" and "night owls"). You need to understand your own circadian rhythm and then, as much as possible, plan your daily routine to conform to it.

Five Ways to Honor Your Body Rhythm

1. Establish a regular pattern.

Many of us live by two distinct patterns, one for the workweek and another for weekends. Perhaps you reward yourself at the end of a tough week with a late Friday night, and you may get up a lot later on Saturday than you do Monday through Friday. Your eating habits may vary considerably, too, especially if you're prone to graze when you're home and near the refrigerator. If the variance is large enough, you may be disrupting your natural rhythms. One reason why you may have an

especially hard time answering the alarm Monday morning
could be because the weekend has thrown you off that rhythm.

To live in harmony with your body, you should ideally get
up from and go to sleep at the same time every day. Night owls
should sleep late, and morning people should get up before the
sun, if that's what comes naturally. But most of us have to
conform to work and school schedules and family demands.
Still, it would be wise to stick to the same pattern every day,
even if it isn't your ideal schedule. I don't want to deprive you
of the exquisite pleasure of sleeping late on Saturdays, but I will
suggest that you coordinate your weekend and workweek
schedules if you have a problem readjusting every Monday.

2. Eat when you're hungry, not when it's "time."

We often eat by the clock, on schedule, thus trampling any
natural sense of when we're hungry and when we're full.
Through custom and the demands of those schedules, many of
us eat little or nothing at breakfast (and perhaps make up for it
with a midmorning donut); eat lunch rapidly, perhaps while
working; and have the big meal at night. We may not have a
leisurely dinner, but we take in a large percentage of our daily
calories at that meal and from late-night snacks.

That probably isn't the way your body wants or needs to be
fueled, however. Nutritionists suggest that the body actually
functions best when we break the overnight fast with a big
breakfast (and yes, fruit and fiber do seem to be the healthiest
choices) and have our lightest meal at dinner. We need the
energy early, and the body metabolizes it efficiently then.
Eating a lot close to the time when we ask our bodies to shut
down for the night makes no biological sense.

3. Take your nourishment in smaller doses.

Folks my age were brought up with the admonition to eat
three square meals a day, a habit that stays with us all our lives.

As we get older and our metabolism slows, we find that snacking makes us gain weight, so we try to discipline ourselves to stop eating between meals. Snacking, grazing, noshing—whatever you call it, most of us feel guilty when we do it.

Turns out this practice is probably all wrong, too. Research now indicates that grazing is a healthier way to eat than packing our entire food intake into one, two, or three meals a day. Diabetics learn to eat several small meals each day; the rest of us should try that, too.

4. Take a siesta.

I'm a short sleeper. I get between six and six and a half hours of sleep most nights, a little more on weekends. Is it enough? Probably not. Science can't really tell me, since it hasn't even figured out why we need to sleep at all, let alone how much sleep we need. I've always gotten up early, even when I stay up late the night before (which doesn't happen often anymore!).

I'm sure that's one reason why I'm such a big advocate of napping. Naps are wonderful. Naps are good for you. Naps are *not* just for the very young and the very old. They are *not* a sign of weakness. (Fatigue, yes, but not weakness.) Naps *are* a chance to get sleep when you need it most and when it will do you the most good. I'll sometimes curl up and take a twenty-minute nap in the middle of a long writing session or just before I start the bike ride home from work. It's remarkably refreshing.

5. Use the rhythm method.

Honor thy peaks and thy valleys.

Try to schedule those activities that require the greatest mental acuity and alertness for your daily peak times, when energy and optimism are high. A valley, on the other hand, is a wonderful time for one of those naps I just mentioned, or at least for those jobs you're able to perform competently while on autopilot.

We have to adjust to the clock, of course, since most of us live in a nine-to-five world. We have to override our bodies' natural desires, but when we do, we pay a price for it. Night owl or morning glory, we all benefit from understanding our body rhythms and adjusting our schedules to accommodate them as much as possible. When you can't control the schedule—the big meeting arrives just as your energy plummets—compensate ahead of time with a longer mini-vacation, perhaps a brisk walk. Compensate, too, by being aware of the source of your reactions. (The boss may not really be completely unreasonable; you're just tired and grouchy.)

First discerning and then honoring your internal rhythms can help you lead a happier, healthier, more productive life.

CHAPTER 15

Making Time

The Substitution Principle of Time Management

You promised to take the family on an outing Saturday. Fact is, you've been looking forward to it. But clanging phones and a last-minute meeting on Friday kept you from finishing your presentation for next Monday. You find yourself in the classic work-or-family squeeze: spend the day with the family, as you want to, or prep for the presentation, as you feel you must.

Whichever you choose, you lose.

Wise time management throughout the week might have headed the problem off. Had you tamed the telephone and e-mail and eliminated or bumped a few of those "urgent but not important" tasks, you might have left yourself an adequate cushion to finish the proposal despite the interruptions, leaving plenty of family time. That doesn't help you now, but the formula in the next section might.

Balancing the Equation

When I took chemistry at John Muir High School, Mr. Browne taught us to balance our equations (something about the valences on both sides of the equals sign needing to come out even). In a sense, that's what the substitution theory of time management is all about. If you're going to take six hours of your weekend finishing the presentation for work, you need to find those six hours to balance the equation. Make a conscious choice: "If this, then not that." Don't simply try to move faster and fit everything in (in essence hoping to expand time), and don't make the choice by default. If you do, family and sleep usually lose.

Remember, you'll never find time—for a family picnic or anything else. You have to make that time by taking it from someplace else, swapping one activity for another.

List all your options, searching first for a way to do both picnic and presentation. What other activities do you have planned or are likely to engage in between now and the presentation on Monday? Perhaps you hope to sleep late on Saturday. You always get in a good vigorous walk before breakfast. You love working the tough Saturday crossword puzzle, and you like to answer your e-mail and spend a little time browsing the Internet. A couple of your favorite TV shows air Saturday night. There's Mass on Sunday, of course, and then brunch and a stroll through the fat Sunday newspapers.

Can you find an easy swap here? The crossword and cruising the Internet are optional, neither urgent nor important, so they're expendable. You can no doubt get everything you really need from the Sunday paper in much less time than you normally take. To find still more time, instead of playing off picnic against presentation, consider substituting picnic for the walk and TV shows. Or you might move a bit of time from several categories rather than taking it all from one.

Sit down with the family, explain the problem, and discuss the options with them. If as a family you can come up with an acceptable swap of time, you've turned a lose-lose situation into a win-win.

Summing Up: Ways to Make Time

By increasing energy and mental focus

- ❍ Take frequent mini-vacations every day.
- ❍ Get proper rest, exercise, and nutrition.
- ❍ Honor your body rhythms.

By organizing more effectively

- ❍ Create and manage to-do lists and other scheduling devices.
- ❍ Eliminate procrastination and reduce startup time.
- ❍ Separate the merely important from the urgent.
- ❍ Follow your own agenda and learn to say no.
- ❍ Tame technology.
- ❍ Stem the information flood.
- ❍ Control the clutter.
- ❍ Turn downtime into productive time.
- ❍ Turn the wait into a rest.

Part Three

Keeping
the Sabbath Holy

CHAPTER 16

The Scriptural and Doctrinal Foundation of the Sabbath

> Do not be afraid to give your time to Christ! (Pope John Paul II, *Dies Domini*, no. 7)
>
> Remember the Sabbath day in order to keep it holy. (Ex 20:8)

In *Dies Domini: On Keeping the Lord's Day Holy*, Pope John Paul II's 1998 apostolic letter, His Holiness calls every Sunday a "little Easter" during which we celebrate the risen Christ, who becomes our nourishment.

"I would strongly urge everyone to rediscover Sunday," he writes. "*Do not be afraid to give your time to Christ!...* He is the One who knows the secret of time and the secret of eternity, and he gives us 'his day' as an ever new gift of his love" (no. 7).

This participating in Mass on Sunday is an opportunity as well as an obligation, as the Church teaches. "Time given to Christ is never time lost," John Paul II reminds us, "but is rather time gained, so that our relationships and indeed our whole life may become more profoundly human" (no. 7).

Sunday is above all an Easter celebration, illumined by the glory of the risen Christ. The biblical foundation for the observance of a day of rest and worship every seventh day goes back to Genesis, where God "rested on the seventh day from all his work that he had done" (2:2). He then "blessed the seventh day and hallowed it" (2:3).

One of the Ten Commandments that Moses brought down the mountain from God instructs us to "Remember the Sabbath day, and keep it holy" (Ex 20:8). "Six days you shall labor and do all your work. But the seventh day is a Sabbath to the Lord your God; you shall not do any work" (Ex 20:9–10).

The Sabbath is to be a day of renewal. It releases us from the burdens of work and helps us recognize our dependence on God. Much more than a mere break from everyday labor, it is to be a celebration of thanksgiving and praise offered in the presence of the living Christ. Every Sunday, as John Paul II tells us, "is the *anastàsimos hemèra*, the day of Resurrection" (no. 19).

Jesus gave the disciples the outpouring of the Spirit on Easter Sunday, and on another Sunday, fifty days after the resurrection, He sent the mighty wind and fire of Pentecost (Acts 2:2–3).Thus, the *Catechism of the Catholic Church* states, "The Sunday celebration of the Lord's Day and his Eucharist is at the heart of the Church's life" (*CCC*, no. 2177). Sunday, the weekly Easter, reveals the meaning of time, pointing toward the day of Christ's coming again.

At the "twofold table of the word and of the Bread of Life," through praying and singing, preaching and listening, we undergo continual conversion, a renewal of our baptismal promises and of the decision to be faithful to God and to obey his commandments (see *Dies Domini*, no. 39).

We partake of the mystery of *kenosis*, the descent by which Christ "humbled himself and became obedient to the point of death—even death on a cross" (Phil 2:8). Our simple lives of work, play, and prayer are united with the life of Christ. We bring all the burdens of the previous six days to the altar.

John Paul II underscores the social as well as the individual benefits of the Sabbath, as it

> [R]esounds through society, emanating vital energies and reasons for hope. Sunday is the proclamation that time, in which he who is the Risen Lord of history makes his home, is not the grave of our illusions but the cradle of an ever new future, an opportunity given to us to turn the fleeing moments of this life into seeds of eternity.... [T]he Church is the companion and support of human hope. From Sunday to Sunday, enlightened by Christ, she goes forward toward the unending Sunday of the heavenly Jerusalem. (no. 84)

At the core of the celebration, of course, is the reception of the sacred Body and Blood of Jesus. "[T]he Church *recommends that the faithful receive communion when they take part in the Eucharist*, provided that they are properly disposed and, if aware of grave sin, have received God's pardon in the Sacrament of Reconciliation" (no. 44).

In the first days of the Church, participating in Mass was voluntary, but the faithful sometimes risked their lives to do it. John Paul II reminds us of the "genuine heroism of priests and faithful ... when faced with danger and the denial of religious freedom" (no. 46).

During the bloody persecution under the Roman Emperor Diocletian that began in A.D. 303, the last and worst of the waves of persecutions of the early Church, many courageous Christians defied the imperial decree. They were willing to die rather than miss partaking in the Eucharist. Diocletian had been relatively liberal toward the Christians, but his subordinate, Galerius, goaded him into his horrible persecutions.

Forty-nine believers in Northern Africa, who became known as the Martyrs of Abitina, asserted that their lives would mean nothing without Christ in the Eucharist. All are believed to have died in prison. Another whole town was wiped out in the frenzy to extinguish the Spirit.

The third-century *Didascalia* urged Christians to "leave everything on the Lord's Day and run diligently to your assembly, because it is your praise of God."

As early as the Council of Elvira, around A.D. 300, and the Council of Agde in A.D. 506, the Church began to speak of "the obligatory character" of the Mass. The *Code of Canon Law* of 1917 gathered this tradition into universal law. The catechism also teaches that "the faithful are obliged to participate in the Eucharist on days of obligation" (*CCC*, no. 2181).

Do you feel obliged to participate in Mass every Sunday and holy days of obligation? Would you go anyway, even if you thought it optional? Do you ever attend Mass when you don't "have to"?

God gave us the Eucharist to nurture and sustain us on the journey. Mass is nourishment for the soul, just as surely as food is nourishment for the body.

The Communal Sabbath:
The Mystical Body of Christ

But what about the claim of those who say, "I can worship God just as well—better, even—by taking a hike through the woods as I can by going to Mass."

I'm sure every priest and CCD teacher has heard this argument many times: "I'm all for God and being good and obeying the commandments, but why should I have to go to Mass?" The rationalization concludes: "Nature is my church."

There's a valid point here. We can surely find God in the rich, complex beauty of his creation. I've given silent thanks and praise at many a mountain lake "cathedral." My wife and I have had the best of both "churches" at once, participating in Masses while gathered at picnic tables in the woods, once while overlooking the confluence of the Mississippi and Wisconsin rivers.

But that doesn't mean I don't also want and need to participate in Mass in church with the assembled faithful. As Pope John Paul II reminds us, we are saved in baptism not as individuals alone but as members of the mystical body, the people of God. It's important, he writes in *Dies Domini*, to come together as "the *ekklesia*, the assembly ... 'to reunite the scattered children of God'" as one body in Christ (no. 31). The Eucharist feeds and forms the Church.

Thus our communion with Christ in the Mass is tied to our communion with our brothers and sisters in Christ. We are "[t]he privileged place of unity: it is the setting for the celebration of the *sacramentum unitatis*," His Holiness tells us, "a people gathered *by* and *in* the unity of the Father, of the Son, and of the Holy Spirit" (no. 36). In these moments, we are in communion with the universal Church worldwide. As we celebrate the Risen Lord together, we are moving toward the eternal feast when the kingdom will be restored.

As we are united in receiving the Eucharist, we are united, too, in the public proclamation of the word and in affirming our beliefs together. Some refer to "preaching to the choir" as a bad or at least unnecessary exercise, since everyone in the choir presumably already believes in the Church's message and is literally singing from the same hymnal. But as every member of that choir knows, our faith requires constant nurturing to deepen and grow. By our presence at Mass, we support one another in our belief, enriching the community with our personal witness.

John Paul II thinks our communal worship is so important, he encourages us to come together for prayer and the word even if no priest is available to preside at a Mass.

CHAPTER 17

The Holy Day of Opportunity—Sabbath as Nourishment and Renewal

The Sabbath is centered on the celebration of the Mass, but it can be much more—and much less. As John Paul II writes: "[T]he Lord's Day is lived well if it is marked from beginning to end by grateful and active remembrance of God's saving work." The Church is "unwilling to settle for minimalism and mediocrity at the level of faith" (no. 52).

We are to keep the Lord's Day not only by worship and prayer, but also by works of mercy, charity, and service, as well as by abstaining from our regular work. That's a tall order, much more than simply "giving an hour to God" at Mass.

Saint John Chrysostom wrote, "What good is it if the Eucharistic table is overloaded with golden chalices, when he is dying of hunger?" (no. 71). The Sabbath is a day for sharing the bounty of God's blessing, of prolonging the miracle of the multiplication of the loaves, as John Paul II suggests, by feeding the hungry. (Of course they may be hungry the other six days of the week, too, but the commitment to share food with them every day flows from the Sabbath impulse.) It's a day to visit those who are isolated by illness, age, or imprisonment, to comfort the afflicted, to work for peace and justice. In this we have the example of Christ himself.

The Fulfillment of the Sabbath in Christ

Christ came to earth, the Gospels tell us, not to abolish the law but to fulfill it. He brought the new wine of the New Covenant, one that would require new wineskins—and new teaching on the law—to hold it. But some of the religious leaders chided Jesus for what they saw as his profaning of the Sabbath.

In Matthew we read of Jesus and his disciples walking through the fields on the Sabbath, plucking heads of grain to eat. Some Pharisees confront Jesus, saying, "Look, your disciples are doing what is not lawful to do on the Sabbath" (Mt 12:2). Jesus reminds them that David once ate "the bread of the Presence, which it was not lawful for him or his companions to eat" (Mt 12:4). And priests, of course, were given the right to "violate" the temple on the Sabbath to perform their priestly duties.

"I tell you, something greater than the temple is here," Jesus then concludes. "For the Son of Man is lord of the sabbath" (Mt 12:6, 8).

Immediately following in Matthew's account, Jesus heals the man with the withered hand, another violation of the law, asserting that "it is lawful to do good on the sabbath" (Mt 12:12).

Again in Luke, we find closely paired Sabbath healings. Jesus is teaching in the synagogue on the Sabbath when he encounters a woman who had been crippled by a demon for eighteen years. "When Jesus saw her," Luke writes (Lk 13:12–13), "he called her over and said, 'Woman, you are set free from your ailment.' When he laid his hands on her, immediately she stood up straight and began praising God."

Imagine that you were there and had just witnessed this miracle!

But the leader of the synagogue was outraged because the healing took place on the Sabbath. Jesus stood his ground and reminded the people that they surely watered their ox or donkey on the Sabbath. "'And ought not this woman,'" he reasons, "'a daughter of Abraham whom Satan bound for eighteen long years, be set free from this bondage on the Sabbath day?'" (Lk 13:16).

Luke's narrative describes another such healing, when Jesus is eating a meal on the Sabbath at the house of a leading Pharisee. A man with dropsy presents himself, and Jesus asks the lawyers and Pharisees if it is lawful for him to heal the man on the Sabbath. When they remain silent, he goes ahead and performs the healing.

"'If one of you has a child or an ox that has fallen into a well,'" he challenges, "'will you not immediately pull it out on a Sabbath day?' And they could not reply to this" (Lk 14:5–6).

What could they say? "Yes, it's all right to violate the Sabbath" or "No, you should not pull your child out of the well"?

Ask those healed of their afflictions. They might tell you that any day is a good day for Jesus to bestow his healing grace on us. By extension, it's always a good time for us to reach out to our brothers and sisters in the love of Jesus. Even on the Sabbath?

Especially on the Sabbath.

Our Sabbath Rest

Mass ends with a sense of mission, the charge to "love and serve the Lord." We are called to bear witness to the world, to be ambassadors of Christ and evangelizers by the way we live:

"present your bodies as a living sacrifice, holy and acceptable, to God" (Rom 12:1).

What we *do* on Sunday matters as much as and possibly more than what we *don't* do. But what we *don't* do matters, too; we are to perform no work on the Sabbath. We need that time and space, instead, to pay more attention to God's creation, in anticipation of the new heaven and the new earth, and to find peace with God, self, and others. Even our good works if done to excess and in frenzy, can hinder us on the spiritual journey.

> The rush and pressure of modern life is a form, perhaps the most common form, of innate violence. To allow oneself to be carried away by the multitude of conflicting concerns, to surrender to too many demands, to commit oneself to too many projects, to want to help everyone in everything, is to succumb to violence. More than that, it is cooperation with violence. The frenzy of the activist neutralizes his work for peace. It destroys his own inner capacity for peace. It destroys the fruitfulness of his own work because it kills the root of inner wisdom which makes work fruitful. (Thomas Merton, *Conjectures of a Guilty Bystander*)

The stricture against laboring on the Sabbath goes back to the core of God's law revealed in Deuteronomy 5:12–14: "Observe the sabbath day and keep it holy, as the Lord your God commanded you. Six days you shall labor and do all your work.... But the seventh day is a sabbath to the LORD your God; you shall not do any work."

It wasn't until the fourth century A.D. that the Roman Empire recognized that people didn't have to work on the day of the sun. Until then, secular law made it difficult and even dangerous to observe the Sabbath. In the nineteenth century, Pope Leo XIII proclaimed that preserving Sunday as a day of rest was a worker's right and that the state was morally bound to guarantee that right.

For those who must work on Sunday (including firefighters and police who labor to keep the rest of us safe), the Church recognizes that the observance of a Sabbath may rightly come on another day of the week.

So-called blue laws once commonly banned the sale of alcohol on Sunday and mandated that certain establishments remain closed. But many people saw such laws as a violation of the separation of church and state (designed at least as much to protect the church from the state as the other way around), and blue laws are rare today.

Many of us refrain from going to the workplace on Sunday but are quite adept at taking our work with us and finding plenty of "homework" around the house. And of course, the shopping malls always beckon. Our culture doesn't offer much to reinforce the notion of a sacred Sabbath. Multiple attractions, distractions, and obligations make it difficult to fully observe the Lord's Day and to keep it holy. It may seem no easier to find time on a Sunday than on any other day of the week.

We need to apply the substitution theory of time management here. We'll never find time for communal worship, for prayer and Scripture reflection, for gathering with family and friends, or for performing acts of charity. We don't *find* time; we *make* time—by not doing all the tasks that occupy and preoccupy us during the other six days of the week.

For me, making time wasn't so difficult. Instead, abstaining from work was my biggest hurdle. For most of my life I justified working on Sunday. For me, labor often involved reading, marking, and grading seemingly endless stacks of student essays, which I balanced on my lap while some sports event played on the television in front of me. And there was always the yard work that I hadn't finished on Saturday.

Only in the last few years have I tried to abstain from all work as part of my Sunday observance. Why the change? I'm not sure. No lightning bolt hit me; I saw no burning bush. I think all the justifying I did for all those years simply wore me down, and I decided to take one of those important next steps along the spiritual journey.

At first it was awful. I'd had to justify the work, yes, but the work had also justified, validated, and defined me. Without it, I couldn't "earn" my rest. I tried to read for pleasure, but it wasn't time yet; pleasure reading was for when the work was done at the end of the day. So I bounced and jiggled and fidgeted, and my skin itched on the inside. Sunday became the longest day of the week.

Slowly that changed; I found a new rhythm, just for Sunday. Now I look forward to my day of rest, when I can treasure the quiet times and actually allow myself to relax and become absorbed in something besides work. The change took place gradually. I'm a slow learner. But now keeping the Sabbath in this new and perhaps fuller way seems natural, and I recognize it as the gift from God that it truly is.

As with all the other commandments, God's admonition to keep the Sabbath holy is designed to help us live more fully, more abundantly in him, so that our joy might be complete. The Sabbath isn't a burden; it's an aid, to help us realize our dependence on God and to receive God's saving grace.

Far from begrudging the Lord his one day in seven, we are to rejoice in it, as we proclaim by thought, word, and deed the new creation, the New Covenant, the risen Christ.

> If you keep my commandments, you will abide in my love, just as I have kept my Father's commandments and abide in his love. I have said these things to you so that my joy may be in you and that your joy may be complete. This is my commandment, that you love one another as I have loved you. (Jn 15: 10–12)

CHAPTER 18

The Case for Daily Mass

Resting and discovering peace on the Sabbath became natural to me only after long weeks of discomfort. So, too, going to weekday Mass started for me as duty, often felt like sacrifice, only after long practice became habit, and then at long last evolved into joy. I now look forward to daily Mass and miss it when deprived of it.

I started going out of despair. My family was experiencing great turbulence, and some days I wasn't sure we'd survive. I went to Mass to plead with God to help us, and to seek solace and peace. Some days I found it; other days, I left feeling worse than when I came. I kept going; I'm not entirely sure why (which is a good indicator of the Spirit at work).

God answered those desperate prayers of mine in ways beyond my longings. Now I usually go to Mass with prayers of thanksgiving and praise in my heart. I hardly dare ask for more than what God has already given me.

For many years I attended the noon Mass at the campus Catholic center right around the corner from my office. I never announced where I was going, of course, but if a colleague asked, I answered honestly.

"Do you go *every* day?" one asked.

"When I can."

"Why? I thought Catholics only had to attend Mass on Sunday."

True, Sundays and those other holy days of obligation: the feasts of the Nativity of the Lord; Mary, Mother of God; the Ascension; All Saints Day; the Assumption of Mary; and the Immaculate Conception (these feasts are obligatory in the United States; in Canada, the holy days are the Nativity of the Lord, and Mary, Mother of God).

But for me, other days have become "holy days of opportunity." Skipping Mass would be like skipping a meal or even not eating all day. Sure, the Sunday dinner might be something special, but I eat on the other six days of the week, too.

Food nourishes my physical body; I get hungry (and cranky) without it. So, too, the word, the Bread of Life, and the cup of salvation nourish my spirit; I feel empty and lost without them. The ritual of breaking bread with my family lifts my spirit and delights my heart; so does coming to the table of our Lord with my fellow believers.

The word uplifts, guides, rebukes, inspires, and informs me, ever new at each hearing. I need that guidance and understanding more than just on Sundays, and I probably need it even more on weekdays, when I'm out and about amid the temptations and diversions of the world.

In short, the Mass sustains me on my daily journey. Now my wife and I attend early Mass at a nearby parish three times a week. In all but the worst weather, we walk, usually seeing one or two commuters standing at the bus stop in front of the church. In summer we walk to and from in dawn's pure light. In winter, we walk or sometimes drive in darkness, often through snow and cold. Somehow it feels even better to go first thing, before eating or working, and it means a lot to me that we worship together.

I don't have to explain to anyone why I go, because the only folks I encounter are the members of a surprisingly large faith community who gather at dawn (or, in winter, before dawn) to worship. I know many by name, most by sight; and I feel a kinship with all.

Long ago I stopped questioning whether I would or would not go to Mass on weekdays (wrestling and rationalizing take a lot of psychic energy) and simply adjusted my schedule and my thinking, making time to accommodate this new activity. Weekday Mass has become a normal and natural part of my routine. Is it difficult to go? Not anymore. What am I missing when I do go? I can't think of anything.

I'm certainly not saying you "should" go to weekday Mass. I am proposing it as an option and offering my personal testimony to how wonderful it can be.

Living on God's Time

We are to live by the Ten Commandments; we have to be careful not to substitute:

The Bogus Ten Commandments

1. Thou shalt be efficient, productive, and rich.

Scour your Bible all you want, you're never going to find texts on time management or quality control. Neither will you find any mention of how to make millions in the real estate market in your spare time while working in your own home.

In fact, despite all those "gospel according to..." rip-offs, God's word makes a lousy business management text—unless your primary business is to seek and live God's will for you.

"[L]oving the LORD your God and walking in his ways always" (Deut 19:9).

The Bible says nothing there about working "smarter not harder," maintaining zero tolerance for error, buying on margin, or leveraging a buyout.

Which brings us to bogus commandment number 2:

2. Thou shalt maximize profits.

Not according to the Man from Galilee. Jesus told the rich man to sell all he had and give the money to the poor. He praised the widow who gave from her needs, not her surplus. He advised to give your coat along with the shirt off your back to the beggar.

Charging exorbitant rates for lending money seems to be pretty strongly frowned on in the Bible, too.

"[B]e steadfast, unmovable, always excelling in the work of the Lord, knowing that in the Lord your labor is not in vain" (1 Cor 15:58).

3. Thou shalt give 110 percent effort to the one who signs your paycheck.

Aside from the mathematical impossibility of there being more than 100 percent of anything, giving everything to the job—in a coach's terms "leaving it all on the field"—leaves nothing for family, friends, charity, worship, Scripture study, or any other worthwhile endeavor God might call you to undertake.

That's not to say you shouldn't work with diligence, concentration, and integrity, delivering that axiomatic "day's work for a day's pay" and perhaps even more. But work must not be the primary focus in your life, no matter how much you justify it as being "for the family." The hardship that accompanies work was originally a punishment, remember. Before that incident with the apple, Adam and Even didn't have to punch a time clock in Eden.

"This is the work of God, that you believe in him whom he has sent" (Jn 6:29).

4. Thou shalt fill every waking moment with activity.

We need to heed the words of the great philosopher Satchel Paige, who once noted, "Sometimes I sit and think. And sometimes I just sit."

"Idle hands are the devil's workshop," goes the old saw, and, like most of our beloved adages, no doubt it has some truth.

But activity for its own sake is not the path to righteousness.

In our culture, it seems to be a crime to get caught doing nothing. Even retirees—who should have earned the right to do a little sitting and cogitating, are constantly urged to get off their duffs and DO SOMETHING!

The Bible, on the contrary, urges us to set aside time to pray—which is by society's definition about as close to doing nothing as you can get. It also urges us to rest, to be quiet so we may hear the still, small voice of God, once the babble of constant doing has subsided.

Remember that Mary sat at Christ's feet while her sister, Martha, did all the work. The Master said Mary had chosen the better portion, and he advised poor, scurrying Martha that one thing only was important. "[S]trive first for the kingdom of God and his righteousness, and all these things will be given to you as well" (Mt 6:33).

5. *Thou shalt multitask.*

Even constant activity is no longer good enough. You must be doing two, three, or even four things at once—if you want to drive yourself crazy while lousing up all the tasks you're trying to juggle.

Two thousand years before modern science began finding evidence to support his contention, a Roman slave named Publilius Syrus had it right: "To do two things at once is to do neither."

Cell phones can deliver stock market quotations, sports scores, and movies. They can even make pictures. No wonder we love to use them while we drive. We're also four times more likely to have an accident if we talk on the cell phone while driving—but now we can at least get pictures of the crash.

Writing for the Web edition of *The Atlantic* in November 2007, Walter Kirn warned about "the monster of multitasking."

Folks who sell us the gadgets that make multitasking so seductive have delivered, according to Kirn, "three inferior substitutes" for freedom: efficiency, convenience, and mobility.

Instead of peace we achieve frenzy, broken only by fatigue.

We have become, Kirn says, "the Federal Reserve of the attention economy, the central bank of overcommitment, keeping the system liquid with adrenaline." Worse yet, we are both banker and borrower, with no way to pay off the debts we owe ourselves.

"Where do you want to go today?" our overwrought lifestyle urges us. To which Kirn replies, "Now that I no longer confuse freedom with speed, convenience, and mobility, my answer would be: 'Away. Just away. Someplace where I can think.'"

In the movie, *Dirty Harry,* Clint Eastwood's Callahan character speaks truth when he says, "A man's gotta know his limitations." Maybe we were only meant to do one thing at a time.

"Rejoice always, pray without ceasing, give thanks in all circumstances; for this is the will of God in Christ Jesus for you" (1 Thess 5:16–18).

6. *Thou shalt amass as much wealth as possible.*

"The one who dies with the most toys wins."

We might not phrase it quite so baldly, but we certainly act as if this were our credo at times. Do we really subscribe to a philosophy so clearly at odds with the teaching of the Bible and the Church?

In business, we work to "maximize profit," charging whatever the market will bear while keeping wages as low as possible. We've built a massive global industry designed solely to manage our wealth, not only to protect it from incursion but also to make it grow.

We do so in the name of providing for our families, being prudent, making sure we'll have enough for retirement—all worthy goals, to be sure. But if we are successful, the question should arise at some point: How much is enough? And is amassing and managing wealth really to be my primary focus and goal in life?

We are a long, long way from Jesus' admonition to the devout young man to "sell all you have and give to the poor," a Scripture passage that makes everyone I know, myself included, very uncomfortable.

"Trust in him at all times, O people; pour out your heart before him" (Ps 62:8).

7. *Thou shalt worship at the altar of oat bran.*

…And offer up sacrifices of tofu, while abstaining from all evil carbohydrates.

Actually, I'm a semi-faithful adherent to the high fiber/low fat way of life. (My wife refers to our typical menu as the "tree bark and prunes diet.") When all the medical specialists seem to line up on the same side, I think it wise to listen to them.

But if we aren't careful, special diets and other self-help regimens can become false gods, tempting us to rely on our own wisdom and works to gain a salvation of sorts (if not eternal life, then at least a longer life on earth). We can become every bit as judgmental toward "nonbelievers" as the members of any religious denomination, sect, or cult toward infidels.

We are not made holy by what we eat. Only God can make us holy. Jesus said, "'[I]t is not what goes into the mouth that defiles a person, but it is what comes out of the mouth that defiles'" (Mt 15:11).

8. *Thou shalt practice all things in moderation.*

…To which the wag might add, "including moderation."

In the ninth century B.C., the historian Hesiod wrote: "Observe due measure, moderation is best in all things." The

Greek playwright Euripides, in *Medea* (about 431 B.C.), called moderation "the noblest gift of heaven." Plato himself advised us to "pursue and practice moderation" (*Gorgias*, about 375 B.C.).

Our culture has embraced the concept—or at least paid lip service to it. To defy the moderation edict, in fact, is to invite public ridicule. Speaking at the Cow Palace in San Francisco in 1964, presidential candidate Barry Goldwater uttered these immortal words: "Extremism in defense of liberty is no vice. Moderation in the pursuit of justice is no virtue." He probably would have lost the election to Lyndon Johnson anyway, but his words, and the vehemence with which he spoke them, were widely quoted as proof of his unfitness to be president and even of questionable mental stability.

But didn't Christ preach a Gospel of total commitment to God's will?

The command to practice moderation in all things never appears in the Bible. It's one of those phantom "scripture" so many of us are sure must be in there somewhere, until we actually try to find it. The Bible does in several places counsel temperance (see 1 Cor 9:25), a more limited concept.

But we are to love the Lord our God with our all our hearts, souls, and minds, holding nothing back.

9. *Thou shalt never give an inch.*

"Winning isn't everything. It's the only thing."

That profundity has been misattributed to former Green Bay Packers coach Vince Lombardi ("St. Vincent" in Wisconsin) for decades. David Marinass, in his definitive biography of Lombardi, *When Pride Still Mattered*, writes that Red Sanders, then head coach at UCLA, said it first.

No matter who said it, it doesn't make a whole lot of sense. But the sentiment is clear: winning *is* everything. It's not how

you play the game that counts, it's whether you win or lose—
or perhaps these days, how much they pay you to play.

My father taught me the opposite—that teamwork, good
sportsmanship, and the ability to lose gracefully—the virtues
we often claim sport teaches us—were much more important
than winning. Not that my dad wasn't fiercely competitive. He
always played to win. But he had his priorities straight.

"Show me a graceful loser," the cynic replies, "and I'll show
you a loser." Our culture encourages ruthlessness in the pursuit
of our often-selfish goals. It teaches us to "stand up for our
rights," to "toot our own horns," and, as the Stamper family
motto succinctly stated in Ken Kesey's great novel, *Sometimes a
Great Notion*, "never give an inch."

No one put this philosophy better than John Wayne, portray-
ing dying gunman John Bernard Books in the movie *The Shootist*:
"I won't be wronged, I won't be insulted, and I won't be laid a
hand on."

I grew up on movies like that; that line, and the man who
said it (while he knew he was dying), still move me.

But I also grew up wanting to be like Jesus, and try as I
might, I could never imagine Jesus responding with words like
that when Judas betrayed him with a kiss and the soldiers
hauled him away to be tortured and crucified.

By word and example, Christ embodies a different sort of
courage. He lived as he believed, that we have nothing to fear
from those who can kill the body but not the soul.

I tried to reconcile my flawed understanding of Jesus with
my internalization of the John Wayne cowboy ethic, but they
just wouldn't blend well. I had to choose, and I've tried to
throw my lot in completely with Jesus and his higher brand of
bravery. Instead of the Code of the West, I'm trying to live by
the Code of Love.

10. Thou shalt follow thy bliss.

"I want it *all!*" an ad currently playing on radio and television thunders. "And I want it *now!*"

Folks who preach that doctrine are usually trying to sell us something that will supposedly make us happy—bliss in a brand or box or on a bandwagon.

Sometimes it's a lifestyle, a political philosophy, or a movement rather than a product, but the implicit promise is the same: do, buy, or believe X and you'll be happy. If you want it—if your heart yearns for it—go for it. Can't afford it? Put it on your credit card. You don't have to worry about it—until the bill comes due.

But the flat-screen TV, the bigger house, the new car, the career—none of them brings peace. They aren't God. Only God is God. There is no other. We pursue God through Scripture, through prayer, through the Eucharist, and through whole-hearted, cheerful giving of ourselves to others, not by getting and spending.

Any "commandment" that tells us otherwise—no matter how compelling or how often-repeated—is a lie.

Somewhere deep inside us, where God has planted his law in us, we know the truth when we hear it. Pursuing that truth will bring that peace that surpasses all human understanding and leads us toward perfect union with God.

The Tin Rule

"God helps those who help themselves."

This is probably the most oft-cited "scripture" never to appear in the Bible.

Go ahead and look for it. I'll wait.

You won't find it among the writings of the Apostle Paul.

He preached the opposite doctrine: "For while we were still weak, at the right time Christ died for the ungodly" (Rom 5:6).

Christ "helped" us by dying for our salvation precisely because we couldn't save ourselves. We live and breathe and have our being in God. Our very conception and birth and our continued existence every moment depend on him.

Have you given up trying to find "God helps those who help themselves"? Try *Poor Richard's Almanac*, published by Benjamin Franklin in 1757. And Franklin lifted it from Aesop's fables.

By adopting a few techniques for managing our time, which is to say our lives, we can free up time and energy to love more fully and joyfully serve God and our family, friends, and neighbors.

Life won't always be easy. Look at the life of the Savior. But ease and comfort, like wealth and prestige, are false gods. If you walk with God, he will "guide you continually, and satisfy your needs in parched places, and make your bones strong; / and you shall be like a watered garden, like a spring of water, whose waters never fail" (Isa 58:11).

In the words of another of God's prophets:

"[W]hat does the LORD require of you but to do justice, and to love kindness, and to walk humbly with your God?" (Micah 6:8).

Sources and Acknowledgements

Value-based time management categories taken from:

Covey, Stephen, A. Roger Merrill, Rebecca R. Merrill. *First Things First*. New York: Simon & Schuster, 1994.

Keathley, J. Hampton, III. "The Stewardship of Time: Multiplying the Life Through Redeeming the Time." Copyright © 1996–2007 by Biblical Studies Press (BSP), L.L.C. and the authors. All rights reserved. Used with permission.

MARSHALL J. COOK taught for the University of Wisconsin-Madison for thirty years and often speaks at conferences nationwide. He has published several books on stress management and has even been a guest on *Oprah* to discuss the topic.

Marshall edits *Extra Innings*, an online newsletter for writers. He has authored thirty books and hundreds of magazine articles. Marshall holds his BA in creative writing and his MA in communications from Stanford University. He has been married to Ellen since 1968, and they have one son, Jeremiah. When not writing, Marshall likes to read, jog, lift weights, and talk back to the television (not all at the same time). He is a passionate minor league baseball fan, drives the back roads, and eats in small town cafes.

Also by Marshall Cook:

How to Handle Worry:
A Catholic Approach

Marshall J. Cook

Today's world is busy and non-stop—one filled with eighty-hour-work weeks and too little time left over. Author Marshall Cook offers a practical approach to deal with the worries and anxieties that creep into our chaotic lives. He explains how we can create and maintain harmony in our lives through faith and prayer. Begin your own journey toward serenity today!

0-8198-3390-8 $12.95

The How to Handle Worry Workbook:
A Catholic Approach

Marshall J. Cook

The How to Handle Worry Workbook directs readers along a path of enlightenment through prayer and reflection. Using step-by-step instructions, Cook guides readers through difficult times, searching for the root of their specific anxieties in order to create personalized management strategies. Cook's trademark humor and reliable expertise make this journal the perfect solution for those struggling with daily worry.

0-8198-3391-6 $10.95

Other titles of interest:

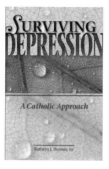

Surviving Depression: A Catholic Approach

Kathryn J. Hermes, FSP

Depression can strike anyone, even those deeply committed to living the Christian life. This reassuring book includes: encouraging stories of others who have lived with depression; psychological, medical, spiritual and practical self-care perspectives; tips for friends and family of the depressed.

0-8198-7077-3 $12.95

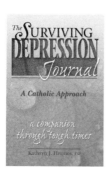

The Surviving Depression Journal: A Catholic Approach

Kathryn J. Hermes, FSP

This companion to the best-selling book, *Surviving Depression*, creates a safe space in which people can journal their struggles and fears and come to a deeper sense of hope, peace, and trust.

0-8198-7104-4 $12.95

Making Peace with Yourself: 15 Steps to Spiritual Healing

Kathryn J. Hermes, FSP

"This is a guide to the deepest reality at work in our lives: God's presence in the midst of life's confusion. "This book explores the stories of people like you and me, people faced with situations that often were irreparable, people who need to make peace with themselves" — *Kathryn J. Hermes, FSP*

0-8198-4859-X $12.95

Order at www.pauline.org, or by calling
Pauline Books & Media at 1-800-876-4463,
or through the book and media center nearest you.

BOOKS & MEDIA

The Daughters of St. Paul operate book and media centers at the following addresses. Visit, call or write the one nearest you today, or find us on the World Wide Web, www.pauline.org

CALIFORNIA
3908 Sepulveda Blvd, Culver City, CA 90230   310-397-8676
2460 Broadway Street, Redwood City, CA 94063   650-369-4230
5945 Balboa Avenue, San Diego, CA 92111   858-565-9181

FLORIDA
145 S.W. 107th Avenue, Miami, FL 33174   305-559-6715

HAWAII
1143 Bishop Street, Honolulu, HI 96813   808-521-2731
Neighbor Islands call: 866-521-2731

ILLINOIS
172 North Michigan Avenue, Chicago, IL 60601   312-346-4228

LOUISIANA
4403 Veterans Memorial Blvd, Metairie, LA 70006   504-887-7631

MASSACHUSETTS
885 Providence Hwy, Dedham, MA 02026   781-326-5385

MISSOURI
9804 Watson Road, St. Louis, MO 63126   314-965-3512

NEW JERSEY
561 U.S. Route 1, Wick Plaza, Edison, NJ 08817   732-572-1200

NEW YORK
64 West 38th Street, New York, NY 10018   212-754-1110

PENNSYLVANIA
9171-A Roosevelt Blvd, Philadelphia, PA 19114   215-676-9494

SOUTH CAROLINA
243 King Street, Charleston, SC 29401   843-577-0175

VIRGINIA
1025 King Street, Alexandria, VA 22314   703-549-3806

CANADA
3022 Dufferin Street, Toronto, ON M6B 3T5   416-781-9131

¡También somos su fuente para libros,
videos y música en español!